South Devon and Dartmoor

Car Tours

John Brooks

Acknowledgements
My thanks go to Josh Brooks who was an invaluable map-reader, and to Heather Pearson and Sandy Sims at the Ordnance Survey for painstakingly checking the text against the maps. I am very grateful to all of them for their support.

Front cover photograph: *Postbridge*
Title page photograph: *Salcombe*

Author: John Brooks
Series Editor: Anne-Marie Edwards
Editor: Paula Granados
Designers: Brian Skinner, Doug Whitworth
Photographs: Jarrold Publishing

Ordnance Survey ISBN 0-3190-0491-0
Jarrold Publishing ISBN 0-7117-0824-X

First published 1995 by Ordnance Survey and Jarrold Publishing

Ordnance Survey
Romsey Road
Maybush
Southampton SO16 4GU

Jarrold Publishing
Whitefriars
Norwich NR3 1TR

Printed in Great Britain by Jarrold Printing, Norwich. 1/95

CONTENTS

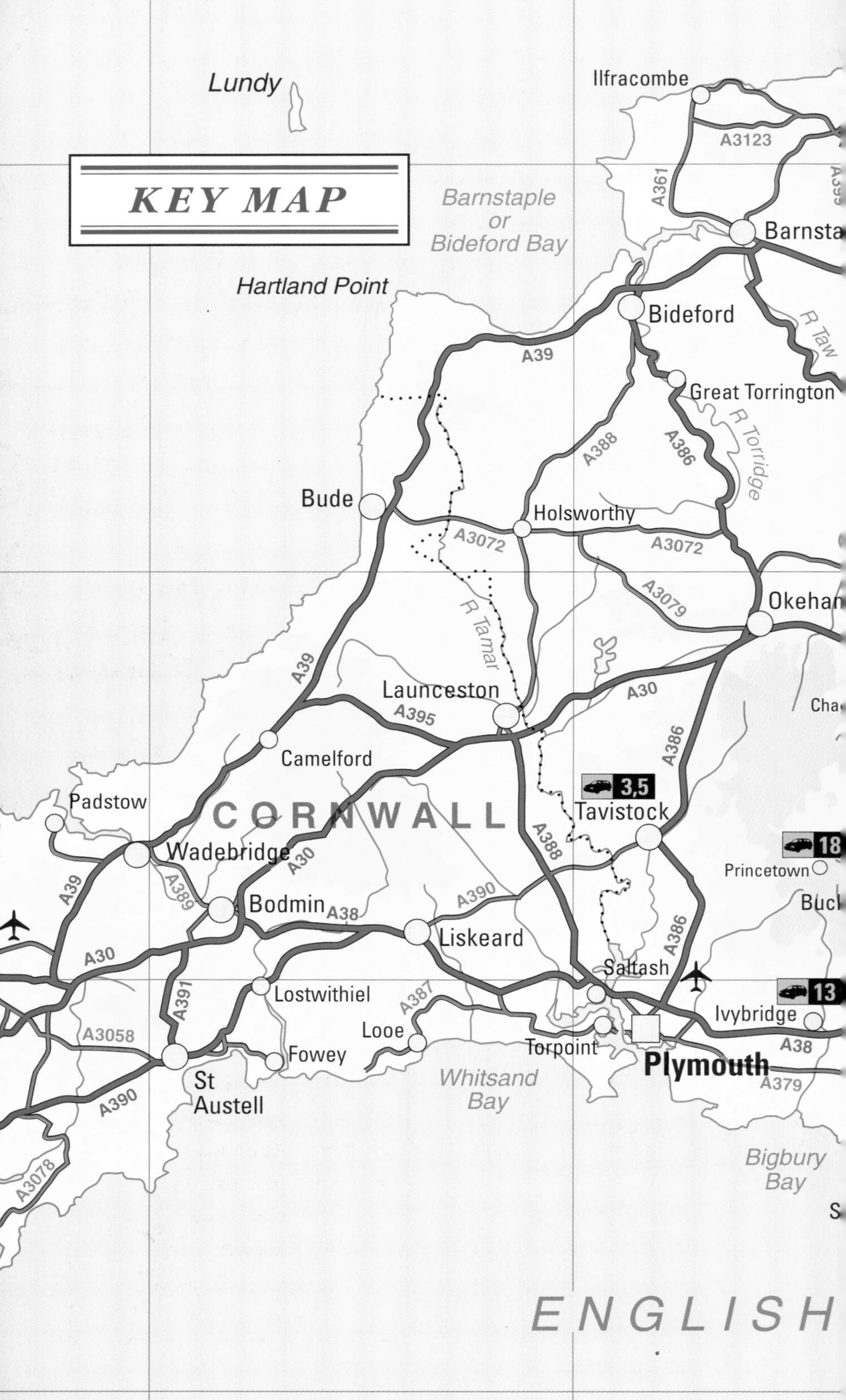
KEY MAP
Lundy
Ilfracombe
A3123
A361
Barnstaple or Bideford Bay
Barnsta
Hartland Point
Bideford
R Taw
A39
Great Torrington
A388
A386
R Torridge
Bude
Holsworthy
A3072
A3072
A3079
Okehan
R Tamar
A39
Launceston
A395
A30
A386
Camelford
3,5
Tavistock
18
Padstow
CORNWALL
Princetown
Wadebridge
A30
A388
A39
A389
Bodmin
A38
A390
Buck
Liskeard
A386
A30
Saltash
13
A391
Lostwithiel
A387
Ivybridge
A3058
Looe
Torpoint
A38
Fowey
Plymouth
A379
St Austell
Whitsand Bay
A390
Bigbury Bay
A3078
ENGLISH

BRISTOL CHANNEL
Weston-super-Mare
Bridgwater Bay
Cheddar
Minehead
Williton
Bridgwater
SOMERSET
Langport
Taunton
Wellington
South Molton
Tiverton
DEVON
Ilminster
Crewkerne
Cullompton
Chard
Crediton
Honiton
Axminster
Exeter
Bridport
Lyme Regis
Seaton
Sidmouth
Moretonhampstead
Bovey Tracey
Lyme Bay
Exmouth
Dawlish
Teignmouth
Babbacombe Bay
Ashburton
Newton Abbot
Torquay
Torbay
Paignton
Totnes
Dartmouth
Kingsbridge
Start Bay
Start Point
CHANNEL
KEY TO MAP
Start of tour
City/major town
Motorway, service area
Junction, limited access
Primary route
Other main road
County boundary
National boundary
0 10 20 30 KM
0 10 20 MILES
1 GRID SQUARE = 40 KILOMETRES

AN INTRODUCTION TO SOUTH DEVON AND DARTMOOR

The landscapes

Devon was the birthplace of many of our greatest seafarers, amongst them the great Elizabethan trio of Hawkins, Drake and Raleigh. The tree-fringed creeks and wide estuaries were ideal places for them to gain the youthful experience which fostered their love for the sea and ships. The coastline of South Devon retains its great beauty. Cliffs shelter broad anchorages created when changes in sea-level flooded the lower reaches of the rivers flowing from Dartmoor. Berry Head separates the more rugged shoreline to the west from the smooth sweep of Lyme Bay to the east which is only interrupted by the red cliffs flanking Tor Bay and then the mouth of the River Exe.

The statue of Sir Francis Drake stands at Tavistock. The greatest of British seafarers was born here c. 1540. He died in 1595 while on a voyage to the West Indies.

Inland, Dartmoor is a dominant feature visible from most parts of South Devon. Its wild and rugged landscape forms a sharp contrast with the surrounding farmland. Here red earth nurtures lush meadows which provide rich grass for the county's famous dairy herds. Few visitors to Devon can resist the temptation of Devon clotted cream! Although Dartmoor's highest point only just tops 2,000 feet (610 m) the climate can be cruel. The craggy tors standing on the summits are the remains of mountains which once stood thousands of feet high and have been worn down by years of weathering.

South Devon's other hills, though less spectacular, are very appealing. To the south of Exeter the Haldon Hills are sandy uplands covered with heath and forest. To the east of the city similar ridges radiate from Cullompton and Honiton. Further to the east are the Blackdown Hills, a lovely area where the wooded hills look down on pastures threaded by sparkling streams and rivers.

The making of the landscape

Devon is the only English county to give its name to a geological period. The Devonian era took place between four hundred and three hundred and fifty million years ago. At this time Devon was

Salcombe and the Kingsbridge estuary from Sharp Tor

situated within an enormous basin of the sea which was being filled by material eroded from the surrounding ranges of mountains. These are the Devonian deposits which were later thrust up from beneath the sea by violent disturbances from within the core of the planet. The heat generated by these events altered many of the rocks physically, converting the basic sandstone into slates, shales and other materials. Some of the earth movements were so violent that the strata was completely upturned, the oldest rock being left on top and the geological sequence reversed.

The geology of the area was further complicated by events which took place in the Carboniferous era which succeeded the Devonian. At this time, about two hundred and ninety million years ago, molten granite was expelled from the earth's core, but was trapped by the overlaying strata. It cooled slowly to form an enormous dome of granite beneath the softer rocks above. In a few places the molten granite escaped to the surface to make spectacular volcanic features such as Brent Tor. In the course of many further millennia the sedimentary rocks above the granite were eroded to leave high mountains. Since then the action of wind, rain and, most tellingly, frost, have worn down the massif into the plateau we know today as Dartmoor. Although only attaining a height of

Torquay, gem of the English Riviera

2,000 feet (610 m), it remains the most formidable tract of high ground in south-west England.

Other, slightly less cataclysmic events also took place. The most violent of these was the earth movement which left Devon with a pronounced tilt to the south. The sea-level was also constantly rising and falling. There was a time when it rose to about 650 feet (200 m) above its present height. It stayed at this level long enough to etch distinct shorelines into the granite of Dartmoor. The sea-level continues to rise today, though whether this is due to the ending of the last Ice Age or to global warming is debatable.

Prehistoric settlement

Man arrived in South Devon about forty thousand years ago (human remains from Kent's Cavern at Torquay have been dated from this time). Later settlers, who lived by hunting, found Dartmoor's breezy plateau safer than the densely-wooded valleys which lay below. These people left little behind them, and the earliest archaeological remains date from the Neolithic era (3500 BC) by which time animals were being herded and crops cultivated. However, most of the prehistoric sites are from the Bronze Age (2000 BC). These include simple burial mounds or barrows, stone rows (whose purpose remains puzzling to experts) and more mundane hut sites. At least five thousand hut sites have been identified on Dartmoor.

During the Iron Age the forest began to be cleared below the moor, and there was further settlement on hilltop sites throughout Devon. The largest of the hill-forts, with a succession of ramparts set closely together, are to be found in the east of the county. Hembury is the finest example, where the defence-works so impressed the Romans when they arrived that they adapted them for their own stronghold.

Devon since Roman times

The Romans adopted Exeter as their outpost in the south-west and built stone walls round the settlement. They provided their legionaries and merchants with a bath house, an emblem of their civilisation. When Roman influence declined, Devon, in common with the rest of the country, spent nearly eight hundred uncomfortable years struggling to emerge from the Dark Ages. However, Christianity was brought to Devon by missionary saints and soon exerted considerable spiritual power. Furthermore, strong links with the continent were established with trade in copper and tin mined from the fringes of Dartmoor. Apart from these civilising influences life must have been a dour experience for the Devonians of the time. Their humble towns and villages were constantly being harried by pirates from Norway and France while a succession of civil wars raged through the area.

Tin Mining

As early as 3000 BC there were tin miners on Dartmoor. This metal, when smelted with copper (also found on Dartmoor), makes bronze, an alloy easily fashioned into weapons or items for domestic use – hence the name of the prehistoric age in which the first miners lived. The demand for tin waned when methods of smelting iron, a more generally available metal, were discovered.

However, in the latter part of the twelfth century copper and tin became important again and towns, dependent on the industry, grew up around Dartmoor. In 1305, Ashburton, Tavistock, Chagford and, a little later, Plympton were made stannary towns (after 'stannum', the Latin word for tin). They were the only places entitled to handle ingots of tin, weighing them for tax assessment and stamping the ingots and coins to validate them. At the same time, tinners were granted special rights since their industry supplied the Crown with substantial revenue. The miners and smelters were considered to be employed directly by the King and were exempted from the normal laws of the land. Special stannary courts inflicted harsh penalties on anyone who hindered the business of the tinners and Lydford Castle became a prision where the transgressors languished.

In late medieval times tin mining declined, but the wool trade grew to maintain the fortunes of the towns which formerly depended on mining. In the nineteenth century tin became important again, and the advent of steam power meant that deeper workings could be exploited. Tavistock was at the centre of this activity, and its fine Victorian buildings were erected as a result. However, the bonanza lasted for a short time, and only a few mines survived into the twentieth century.

The arrival of the Normans, though they dispossessed many of the Saxon estate owners, at least brought a period of peace and stability. In the Middle Ages the rearing of sheep brought unexpected wealth into the towns and villages and magnificent churches were built, or existing ones embellished. It is possible to be cynical about this today, and believe that the medieval tycoons were laying up treasure for themselves in heaven as well as on earth but, hopefully, the result of their efforts proved to be as pleasing to God as it has been to succeeding generations. From the great cathedral at Exeter and wonderful town churches like those at Cullompton or Ottery, to humble ones in villages such as Doddiscombsleigh, there are enduring beauties to be seen and treasured.

One of the remote antiquities of Dartmoor – the stone circle below Little Hound Tor

The old manors and farmhouses concealed in remote valleys beneath sheltering hills shed light on another aspect of our heritage. The history of many of these properties, and sometimes the fabric too, goes back to the time of the Domesday Book. Often they have been the homes of the same family for many generations, and the local parish church will have memorials which chronicle their successes and misfortunes. These houses were the homes of owners of large farms and small estates. Devon's thatched cottages, usually inhabited today by the comparatively well-off, were once occupied by

The churches of Dartmoor were built with wealth generated by the wool trade

Kingsbridge harbour is always busy

poor labourers and yeomen smallholders. Although considered picturesque nowadays, in the past they were often damp and uncomfortable. Thatch was an unreliable and dangerous method of roofing. In one of his short stories Henry Williamson wrote:

The thatch of Frogstreet farmhouse was so old and rotten that docks, nettles and grass grew out of the clumps of green moss on it. Oat sprays grew every summer, too, near the base of the chimney stack...Rain went right through the remains of seven thatchings – the thatch was relaid four or five times every century, and the oat berry which sprouted and started a colony beside the chimneystack of Frogstreet farmhouse must have lain dormant in the roof for more than a hundred and sixty years.

Fires frequently destroyed buildings roofed with straw. Nearly all of south and mid-Devon's major towns were burned down at one time or another. In the eighteenth century Crediton suffered from regular fires. On one such occasion four hundred houses were destroyed. This explains the absence of medieval and Tudor buildings from their streets.

Devon's roads developed from the pack-horse trails used to take wool and finished cloth to the small ports scattered around the coast.

This thatched cottage is at Waddeton, near Brixham

Until the coming of turnpike roads long-distance travel over land was an expensive and tiring business using tracks only suitable for those on foot or horseback. Some villagers in remote areas of Dartmoor lived into the nineteenth century without seeing a wheeled vehicle! The advent of rail travel in the mid-nineteenth century opened up the west of England to commerce and to tourists.

Devon today

Devon's coastline has a string of famous resorts which are colourful and bustling places in the summer. Many of them grew from being small bathing-places in the eighteenth and nineteenth centuries when European wars meant that wealthy people could not tour abroad. Much of Dartmoor also earns a livelihood, or at least a subsidy, from tourism. The districts around Exeter and Plymouth are busy at any season as these cities are the main commercial and industrial centres of the area. Apart from agriculture and tourism they generate the greatest part of the county's wealth. This leaves an enormous expanse of countryside which can only be described as 'unspoilt'. Narrow twisting lanes lead past ancient farms and thatched cottages. Tall-towered churches overlook meadows and wooded valleys. These are the hidden places of Devon which are often only discovered by accident when you have misread a map or are attempting a diversion to avoid traffic. Some of the routes in this book will take you to such beauty spots as well as more famous ones. The byways which take you there are beautiful, often high-banked, and are colourful with primroses, daffodils or foxgloves.

Seasons are important to the visitor to Devon. The seaside resorts are naturally busiest in high summer, and the roads around them are often congested at this time. However, at most other times the roads are comparatively free of traffic. It is possible to find spaces in car parks enabling you to visit beauty spots or explore the countryside on foot.

The climate of South Devon is benign in winter and, if you choose a dry day, most of the drives will be just as enjoyable at this time of year. Spring comes early to these parts, except on Dartmoor where winter can easily linger into the weeks around Easter. Fresh greenery makes early summer a colourful time of the year but, most spectacular, is the splendour of the autumn foliage. The days may be short, but you will find the radiant colours, combined with a low sun, give the scenery an extra dimension.

ENJOY YOUR TOUR

Please read through the tour before starting and, if visibility is poor when you intend to set out, reject those offering fine panoramas from lofty viewpoints. Hopefully, you will find a neighbouring route which visits historic buildings or towns where there are shops and museums. All tours are circular so they can be started at any point. To make the routes easier to follow the navigational instructions have been printed in bold. There are also boxed letters which tie in with those on the map. Their purpose is to aid your navigation and, in many instances, highlight sections of the route requiring particular attention. The times given for each tour cover motoring only but, if you decide to explore footpaths or visit attractions, they can easily take the best part of a day. It is possible that opening times for the various attractions may have changed, and it is advisable to telephone before visiting. If you plan more extensive walks the Pathfinder guides or the Pathfinder maps at 1:25 000 (2½ inches to 1 mile/ 4 cm to 1 km) are ideal – for details see inside back cover.

Devon lanes are notorious for their high banks and tortuous bends. They can also be very steep and narrow. It is always best to anticipate there being a milk tanker or kamikaze delivery driver approaching blind corners from the opposite direction! In a few instances the routes pass through fords which are usually easy to cross but may prove hazardous after exceptional rainfall or at high tide. Alternative ways are suggested to circumvent these. If you are sightseeing on a single-track road, pull over as often as possible to allow following traffic to pass.

• TOUR 1 •

MORETONHAMPSTEAD, BOVEY TRACEY AND WIDECOMBE IN THE MOOR

36 MILES – 2½ HOURS
START AND FINISH AT MORETONHAMPSTEAD

This is a drive full of surprises. Mardon Down, within two miles of the start, is a beautiful heathy area providing a grand overall view of Dartmoor. A little further on Blackingstone Rock rises abruptly out of the landscape like a Dartmoor version of Ayers Rock. The latter part of the tour takes you through better-known countryside, and visits Widecombe and North Bovey, villages famous for their beauty.

Moretonhampstead is on the edge of Dartmoor where the main road across the moor (B3212) meets the one skirting its north-eastern edge (A382). The Bowring Library and the war memorial mark the centre of the town with the parish church at the end of a short cul-de-sac to the right.

The route starts by taking the lane opposite the entrance to the library, Lime Street, which has a lamp standard in the middle of a traffic island. The lane quickly leaves the town and climbs steeply heading for Mardon Down. **After about 1 mile it crosses a cattle-grid and divides. Bear left towards Clifford Bridge and then fork right, almost immediately, on to a minor road signposted to Small Ridge.** There are fine views from here over open countryside, and these are even better if you leave the car and climb to the top of the bracken-covered down.

Keep straight on when a road leaves to the right signposted to Exeter and Hennock. The road becomes very narrow as it drops ever more steeply. There is a camp site just before the bridge across the River Teign. **Turn right to cross the bridge and right again at the following crossroads A to Dunsford.** The road runs by the

• PLACES OF INTEREST •

Moretonhampstead
The town's position at the point where five roads meet made its market important, but its early prosperity came mainly from the wool trade. This is reflected in the graceful granite tower of its church which dates from 1418. The other notable buildings are the almshouses built in 1637. They have a colonnade with tubby granite columns which, fortunately, survived a disastrous fire in 1845 which destroyed much of the town. The almshouses are situated just below the church.

During the Napoleonic wars French officers were allowed to live at Moreton (as locals refer to the town) rather than being confined in Dartmoor prison. They entertained the townspeople on 19 August 1807 by playing music at the church gate. People danced on a platform built in a great elm tree which once stood close by. Today, Moretonhampstead's colourful carnival takes place at the end of August. It is pleasing to think that these festivities originate from the way in which the French prisoners made the most of their misfortune.

Parke Rare Breeds Farm, Bovey Tracey
Set in beautiful parkland, the farm is stocked with old breeds of animals which were kept in medieval days, and whose ancestors roamed the country in prehistoric times. Cattle, sheep, goats and pigs can be seen in the fields, while poultry occupy the old, walled garden of Parke. This mansion is the headquarters of the Dartmoor National Park.

Entry to the National Trust's land here is free, and there are waymarked walks through the woods and by the river. However, the farm is privately run and an admission charge is made. A covered farmyard allows the animals to be seen in wet weather. Refreshments are available. Open April–October daily 10–5 (last admission 4).

river for a short distance before swinging away to the left. A footpath continues through the valley, and this makes a lovely walk, especially in the spring when parts of the riverside are ablaze with daffodils. Rather than leave your car on the side of the road it is advisable to continue to the car park at Steps Bridge (see below) and walk the short distance back.

The lane leads to Dunsford, a village famous for its beautiful thatched cottages. Pass the village hall, pub, post office and church, and keep on the main road through the village to descend to the Exeter-Moretonhampstead road. **Turn right here and pass the Dunsford Mills Hotel to come to Steps Bridge.** There is a car park and National Park Information Centre to the right of the road. Opposite there are footpathes and nature trails in Bridford Wood, a beauty spot cared for by the National Trust.

Keep on the main road to continue up the richly-wooded valley of the River Teign. **About 1 mile from Steps Bridge turn left B on to a narrow lane signposted to Westcott. Be prepared to make a very sharp turn to the left just before Lower Westcott Farm.** After this the lane climbs very steeply. At the top of the hill Heltor Rock can be see to the left. **At a junction turn right (away from the rock) to head towards Moreton.** The road dips and rises before reaching another impressive granite tor, Blackingstone Rock C. There is a parking place for visitors on the left. You have to walk across another lane to reach the rock which stands 80 feet (24 metres) high. The top is reached by steep steps on the north-eastern side which were put there in Victorian times. It provides a magnificent panorama over Dartmoor where, on a good day, many of the most distinctive tors can be picked out. To the east there are views towards Haldon Forest.

A few yards further along the lane turn sharply left to Christow and pass another

SCALE 1:250 000 OR 1 INCH TO 4 MILES *1 CM TO 2.5 KM*

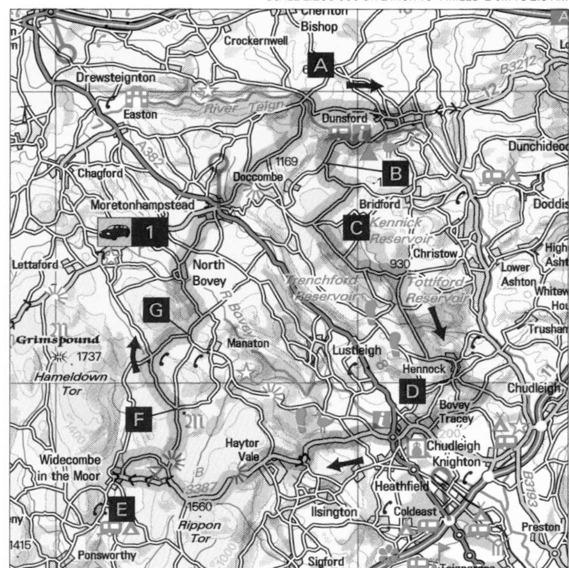

Widecombe in the Moor – its church is known as 'The Cathedral of the Moor'

North Bovey, with its village pump on the green, is one of the prettiest of Dartmoor villages

parking place close to the south side of the rock. There are wonderful views to the right as the road passes through an avenue of beech trees.

Keep straight on past a turn to the left to Bridford and a later turn to the right to Hennock and Bovey Tracey. The three reservoirs (Kennick, Tottiford and Trenchford) are very popular with fishermen. Their banks are covered with rhododendrons and are particularly beautiful during early summer. The road crosses the dam which divides Kennick and Tottiford reservoirs.

After crossing the dam take the first turning to the right to Bovey Tracey. The lane descends into a wooded valley and comes out at Cherrycombehead. Turn left into Hennock. The pub here boasts of its panoramic views. **Turn right to pass the post office and head for Chudleigh and Bovey Tracey. A most complicated junction follows D at Five Lanes. Keep on the main road here by turning left towards Bovey Tracey. Pass Frost Farm and turn right at Little Hillstone Bench, still following the signs to Bovey Tracey. There are many twists and turns and ups and downs before the road passes a cemetery and meets the B3344. Turn right on to this main road and follow it past the church into the centre of Bovey Tracey following signs to Newton Abbot.**

On the far side of the town, after the main car park, go straight over a roundabout by the fire station on to the B3387 following signs to Manaton and Widecombe in the Moor. Pass a large car park on the left. Keep straight on at the roundabout by the fire station. Parke is on the right-hand side, and is the headquarters of Dartmoor National Park. The National Trust owns the parkland surrounding the mansion in which the National Park offices are situated. There is also a privately-operated Rare Breeds Farm.

Shortly after the driveway to Parke bear left keeping on the B3387 to Haytor and Widecombe. The road passes the Edgemoor Hotel and climbs steadily. After a cattle-grid it

• PLACES OF INTEREST •

Haytor Rocks

Because it is so close to the road this is the most visited of any Dartmoor tor. Its summit stands at almost 1,500 feet (457 m) and provides an excellent viewpoint over Dartmoor and its surroundings. The quarries to the north of Haytor provided granite for many of Britain's most prestigious buildings, including the pillars of the British Museum. In 1820 the owner of the quarries, George Templer, built a remarkable railway from the quarries down to the canal his father had constructed twenty-five years previously. The quarried stone then went to the docks at Teignmouth. Templer used granite sets instead of rails, a flange cut from each length of stone keeping the wagons on the tracks. This track, and even the ingenious points which were used when two lines met, may still be seen on Haytor Down.

A heritage trail, known as the Templer Way, leads from the quarries down to the Teign estuary.

North Bovey

This village is one of the most attractive on Dartmoor. Delightful cottages surround a green with the church on one corner and the pub on another. The latter is older than the church, dating from the thirteenth century. The church was built about two hundred years later, and has many details which will intrigue the connoisseur of fine churches. The bosses on the roof of the chancel are particularly interesting. One appears to show three rabbits with their ears joined. A variety of explanations have been offered to explain this carving. One suggests that it is a secret symbol connected with alchemy only known to the brethren of tin miners whose money helped build the church. Another proposes that the ears are those of hares, an animal which was considered to have magical qualities. At the end of harvest a corn dolly, in the shape of a hare, would often be left in a field to promote fertility. Alternatively, the three animals may represent the Trinity, though this would appear to be rather disrespectful.

reaches open moorland and there is a good view of Haytor Rocks ahead. There are several car parks to choose from if you wish to climb to the top of the rocks, or reach the summits of Saddle Tor or Rippon Tor (the latter is to the left of the road). The road climbs steadily, and obviously the higher the parking place the less demanding your ascent on foot will be!

Dunsford is situated on the northern edge of Dartmoor

Continue ahead on the B3387 at Harefoot Cross towards Widecombe. You will soon see the church in its memorable setting as you descend into the village. There are tea shops, pubs and an information centre.

Retrace your route eastwards from the village but, immediately before the bridge E, take the well-concealed lane on the left. The road follows the stream and then crosses it to climb steeply to the top of Bonehill Down. This hill provides some wonderful places for picnics. There are fine views, especially northwards towards Hound Tor.

Turn left at the road junction and continue to Swallerton Gate F. There is a car park for those wishing to climb Hound Tor. **Bear left here towards Chagford.** Jay's Grave may be seen just before a group of Scots pines on the left, about a mile from the junction. Mary Jay was buried in this lonely spot about two hundred years ago. She found herself to be pregnant and committed suicide. The grave always has a posy of flowers on it.

At the following cross-roads, Heatree Cross, turn right towards Manaton. This narrow enclosed lane can be quite busy in the summer, and the passing places are screened by bracken. **Ignore a turn to the left to Barracott and, when the road swings right towards Manaton and Becka Falls, keep straight on G towards North Bovey.** There are a pair of old bridges to cross before the lane reaches the village. The car park is to the right and the church to the left as you approach the green.

Continue on the main road towards Moretonhampstead, entering the town past playing fields. Turn right on to the B3212 to reach the starting point of the tour. ■

Blackingstone Rock is easily climbed and makes a wonderful viewpoint

• TOUR 2 •

CHAGFORD, OKEHAMPTON AND THE TARKA TRAIL

53 MILES – 3 HOURS
START AND FINISH AT CHAGFORD

This drive starts by skirting Dartmoor, giving vistas of its loneliest heights, before reaching Okehampton. From here the tour explores an area of mid-west Devon. The beautiful landscape is principally dedicated to dairy farming. Try to find time to visit Castle Drogo before returning to Chagford. The castle dates from 1910 so is far from being an ancient stronghold, but is nevertheless a remarkable building giving an excellent insight into Edwardian life.

At the top end of Chagford market-place (with the church to the left) turn right on to the road to Gidleigh and Throwleigh. The road divides before leaving Chagford. Fork right here, still heading for Gidleigh. Bear right at a crossroads to cross the ancient bridge and then turn left to Murchington and Gidleigh. At a major road keep straight on, again heading towards Gidleigh. Keep on the main road past Murchington Cross. After passing through lovely woodland the road climbs steeply to a junction. **Turn right into the village of Gidleigh to pass the church and the castle. Turn left at the following junction towards Scorhill and Creaber.**

Drewsteignton lies at the heart of excellent walking country

There are only scant remains of Gidleigh Castle, which was built for Sir William Prous in the late thirteenth century. The Mariners' Way leaves the road northwards opposite the church. This is a long-distance footpath which once enabled sailors, when changing ships, to walk from coast to coast. If you follow the Mariners' Way southwards from Gidleigh you will wind your way down through beautiful woods to a bridge over the North Teign River and then climb to the moor. It passes the ruins of a tiny medieval chapel,

• PLACES OF INTEREST •

Chagford

Chagford may seem like a charming little backwater today but, as one of Dartmoor's three original stannary towns (the others being Tavistock and Ashburton, with Plympton being added later), it had considerable importance in the Middle Ages. This is reflected in its large church. One roof boss shows the three dancing rabbits, an emblem of the tinners. One of the best features of the church is the tomb of Sir John Whiddon who died in 1575. Mary Whiddon, his descendant, was shot in the church on her wedding day by a rejected suitor.

Chagford was also important for its woollen industry. Its mills survived until the middle of the nineteenth century, though the water-wheel of the last mill was put to good use – it was coupled to a generator and supplied the town with electricity, making Chagford the first place west of London to enjoy such a luxury. Ironically, its delightful market-house was built shortly after the last mill closed.

Another violent episode from Chagford's past occurred in the porch of the thatched Three Crowns Inn which stands opposite the church. In 1643 young Sidney Godolphin, cavalier-poet, was shot 'somewhat above the knee' and 'died on the instant, leaving the misfortune of his death upon a place which could never otherwise have had a mention in the world' (Clarendon).

SCALE 1:250 000 OR 1 INCH TO 4 MILES *1 CM TO 2.5 KM*

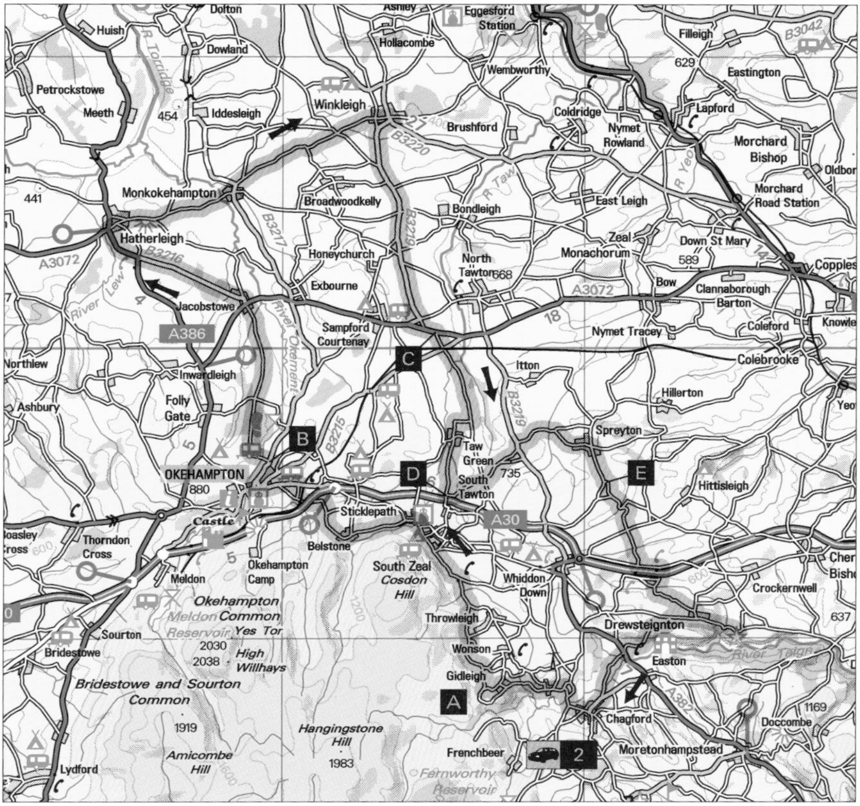

almost completely hidden by undergrowth. The chapel was abandoned after 1328 when its priest was brought to trial for 'maltreating Agnes, daughter of Roger of Gidleigh Hall, and getting her with child'. As this seduction took place at the chapel it was considered desecrated and soon became derelict.

At the next junction A turn right on to a road signposted to Moortown and Ensworthy. Follow this lane round to the left at Moortown Cross and cross a cattle-grid on to open moorland. There are places to park by the roadside here. You may like to picnic or climb Buttern Hill or Rival Tor, both excellent viewpoints. **Keep ahead when successive roads leave to the right. Turn left at a major road coming from Throwleigh.** If you wish to visit the picturesque village of South Zeal take the slip road off to the left immediately before the junction with the main road.

To continue the tour turn left on to the main road. This road leads into Sticklepath where the chief attraction is the National Trust's Finch Foundry, a working museum of waterpower.

At the end of Sticklepath turn left on to a lane, signposted to Skaigh, which leads to Belstone. This remote moorland village is popular with walkers – the famous Tarka Trail passes through it. The route, which covers 180 miles,

The sixteenth-century Fingle Bridge spans the River Teign

Chagford's delightful market-house marks the centre of the village

commemorates Henry Williamson's famous book *Tarka the Otter*. Belstone is close to the southernmost point of the trail which leads to Ilfracombe and Lynton in the other direction.

Belstone church is hidden behind the Tors pub to the left of the road. **At the end of the village there is a most ambiguous road sign. The dead-end is the road ahead, so turn right here on to the lesser road.** This lane leads you into Okehampton, going beneath the bypass. **Turn right after a railway bridge and then left when you meet the B3260 to descend the hill into the town centre.** The Museum of Dartmoor Life is to be found next to the Tourist Information Centre. The Victoria Arcade is an early example of a shopping precinct.

Okehampton Castle is haunted by the shape of Lady Howard, who is supposed to have murdered four husbands, and by a black dog whose glance brings death to anyone unfortunate enough to receive it. The ruins of the twelfth-century stronghold are reached via George Street which brings you to Castle Lane.

From Okehampton take the road north to Exbourne via Northfield Road. This is a one-way street leaving the main road opposite pink-washed flats with ornate balconies. At the end of the road turn right on to the Exbourne road (B3217). This is a one-way street at first. It leads through an industrial estate before suddenly becoming a country lane. **Take the first turn to the left B on to a lane to Hook and cross the River Okement.** The lane winds up steeply through woods, and there are good views from the top. Abbeyford Woods have a picnic place and forest walks.

Go straight over the cross-roads at the end of the woods. The road is now a quiet country byway with gateways allowing wide views over the countryside.

The lane meets the A3072 at Jacobstowe. Turn right here and then immediately left towards Hatherleigh. Pass the church on the left. The road goes through an avenue of beech trees and passes the parkland of Broomford Manor. **After a little more than 2 miles it reaches the A386 at Basset's Cross. Turn right to come to Hatherleigh.** This is a small market town which has seen little change since being rebuilt after disastrous fires in 1840 and 1846. **If you do not wish to explore Hatherleigh continue past the Bridge Inn and then take the first turning to the right to Monkokehampton.**

There are views of the church and buildings as you climb out of the town. Within a mile you come to the Hatherleigh Monument. This commemorates Lieutenant Colonel William Morris, a local man who distinguished himself in the Charge of the Light Brigade at the Battle of Balaclava in 1854. From this viewpoint many features of Dartmoor can be identified – amongst them High Willhays, at 2,038 feet (621 m), the highest point on the moor. The fine views continue after the monument until the road dips down to cross a bridge over the River Okement and enters Monkokehampton. There is an old mill on the right after the bridge and the church is to the left. **Turn left at the post office towards Winkleigh. At the end of the village, after another bridge, turn right off the main road again heading towards Winkleigh.**

This quiet lane crosses a charming stretch of countryside to reach Winkleigh. The hilltop village had castles in the twelfth century – Croft Castle at one end and Court Castle on the other (northern) side. The church is outstanding for its colourful Victorian interior. **Go straight over at Townsend Cross to the village centre. Turn right on to the B3220 and then immediately right again to take the B3219 towards Broadwoodkelly and North Tawton. At Culm Cross**

Hatherleigh is a little town well away from the beaten track

• PLACES OF INTEREST •

Museum of Waterpower (Finch Foundry), Sticklepath. This unique factory was closed in 1960, but it was rescued by the National Trust who restored it to its original appearance. Three water-wheels provided power to drive great hammers, shears, grindstones etc. which helped to make the hand tools produced at the foundry. Open Easter–October Mondays–Saturdays 10–5 (also Sundays 10–5 in July and August). Telephone: (0187) 840046.

Okehampton
There was a Saxon settlement near the site of the modern town before Baldwin de Brionne, the Norman overlord of Devon, built his castle in 1086. In 1170 the stronghold passed to the Courtenay family. They held it until 1538 when Henry Courtenay, Marquess of Exeter, fell foul of his cousin, Henry VIII, and lost his head as well as his castle. The Norman stronghold was remodelled in the fourteenth century to provide more comfortable living quarters as well as better defences. After the Courtenays' fall from favour the castle was neglected and gradually became a romantic ruin, now cared for by English Heritage.

Okehampton has been transformed by the building of the modern bypass. It has good shops and recreational facilities.

Okehampton Castle. Open all year. April–September daily 10–6. October–March Tuesdays–Sundays 10–4. Telephone: (01837) 52844.

Museum of Dartmoor Life, West Street. The museum, with craft workshops and tourist information centre, are housed in a complex based on a former water-mill. It has displays illustrating many aspects of life in the district, including reconstructions of tin and copper mines. Open Easter–October Monday–Saturday 10–5 (and Sundays June–September). Telephone: (01837) 52295.

Castle Drogo, Near Drewsteignton
This must be the most remarkable of all National Trust properties. It is a large country house built between 1910 and 1930 by Sir Edwin Lutyens for Julius Drewe, founder of the Home and Colonial Stores. He was able to retire with a fortune at the age of thirty three.

Despite great misgivings, Lutyens managed to fulfil his commission, combining medieval features, including granite walls 6 feet (1.8 m) thick, with luxuries such as an internal telephone system and electricity generated by turbine. The domestic details such as the bathrooms, larders and kitchen are very interesting but, most amazing, is that this vast and impregnable structure was built in the twentieth century.

Open April–October daily except Friday 11–5.30. Telephone: (01647) 433306.

turn right and then left on to the A3072.

After 1/2 mile (just beyond Spires Lakes) there is an unsignposted road to the right C. Take this to cross the B3215 by turning right and then left after the railway bridge, following signs towards Taw Green and South Tawton. The road crosses the infant River Taw over a narrow humpbacked bridge. **About 3 miles after this turn right and follow the major road to reach Taw Green, rejoining the Tarka Trail. Keep straight on at the next junction.** Pass a telephone-box, cross a small bridge and then pass the imposing entrance to Wood House on the left.

Just before the bridge over the A30 turn left D to Spreyton. The road narrows and passes through dense woodland. **Go straight over the cross-roads at Spitlar Cross. When the road divides bear left around a triangle of woodland. Continue over the B3219 by turning left and then right. Cross a humpbacked bridge and then fork right to reach Spreyton.** Tom Cobley, who rode his grey mare the 15 miles to Widecombe Fair, is buried in the churchyard. **Turn right on to the main road at the end of the village heading towards Whiddon Down. After less than a mile look for a turn to the left E to Falkedon. At the next junction keep ahead towards Hittisleigh. Follow the road down to cross a shallow ford. Bear right after the ford and climb the hill to the crossroads. Go straight on towards Fursham.** After this the road descends again between steep banks. **When you meet the Whiddon Down to Crockernwell road, turn left along the road which runs parallel to the A30. After 1/2 mile, turn right to pass beneath the main road (even though there is a sign to Castle Drogo straight ahead). You are now heading for Drewsteignton. Turn right at Netherton Cross into the village. Continue past the square and then turn right to Castle Drogo and Chagford.**

However, you may like to divert down the road to the left after the church which goes to Fingle Bridge. This detour will allow you to see the sixteenth-century pack-horse bridge and enjoy wooded walks in the narrow, precipitous valley of the River Teign.

The grand entrance to Castle Drogo is about a mile out of the village on the left. After this the road dips into the valley. **Cross the A382 at Sandy Park to come to a beautiful old bridge across the River Teign and so return to Chagford.** ■

• TOUR 3 •

PRINCETOWN AND BURRATOR RESERVOIR FROM TAVISTOCK

35 MILES – 2 HOURS
START AND FINISH AT TAVISTOCK

The towers of the churches at Mary Tavy and Peter Tavy are prominent moorland landmarks. The beautiful River Tavy is crossed at Hill Bridge and then quiet country lanes are used to reach the road over the moor to Princetown, where a visit to the High Moorland Visitor Centre will help you appreciate Dartmoor's history, both natural and man-made. The return to Tavistock is via Burrator Reservoir where there is a choice of delightful picnic places as well as walks to please the energetic climber or the after-lunch stroller.

Take the A386 road north-eastwards out of Tavistock, heading for Okehampton. Pass Kelly College, a leading independent school. **A road to Peter Tavy goes off to the right about 2½ miles out of town – do not take this. Continue for another mile and then turn right at the Mary Tavy Inn on to the road signposted to Mary Tavy church and Horndon A.** The road descends steeply to a small bridge. The church is situated on the cul-de-sac to the right.

Take the next road to the right to Horndon. It climbs quite steeply past the very isolated Elephant's Rest pub (did such a beast ever pause to take breath here?). Above Horndon the road comes to open moorland and there are extensive views to the right. After a second cattle-grid the way becomes enclosed and narrow. **Keep on the main road when a road goes off to the left to Willsworthy and Lane End** (where there is a car park for those wishing to explore the upper reaches of the Tavy valley and the tors which overlook it). The road, now really a lane, drops down steeply to Hill Bridge, a charming beauty spot

• PLACES OF INTEREST •

Tavistock

Few towns have had their history better chronicled than Tavistock. The town belonged to the Benedictine Abbey from 974 until the dissolution of the monasteries in 1539. Thus, it was fortunate to grow in the shade of the monastery, one of the wealthiest in the west of England. After the dissolution, the town became part of the estate of the Duke of Bedford, and remained so until 1911.

As part of the Bedford estate its success was even greater. Just as the abbey had seen the town prosper from the wool trade as tin mining on Dartmoor had declined, so the Duke of Bedford was able to promote copper mining in succession to cloth making.

In the nineteenth century the Dukes proved to be enlightened landlords. They built commodious housing for the miners, laid out the centre of the town, and put up handsome public buildings. The result is that Tavistock is one of the most appealing of all English market towns. Nothing remains of its once great abbey, apart from the gatehouse, restored by the sixth Duke to serve as the town's library, and Betsy Grimbal's Tower, a smaller gatehouse which is supposed to take its name from a lady who was killed on its stairs by a soldier. Her ghost is seen if calamity is about to strike the country.

Tavistock's parish church is dedicated to St Eustace. It dates from 1318, though it was extensively enlarged in the early sixteenth century. This reflected the prosperity that its citizens had gained from the wool trade. It has excellent Victorian glass, some by William Morris.

St Eustace's Church at Tavistock, a church built in the grand manner with money from the wool trade

with riverbank footpaths.

Drive up the hill from the bridge and turn right at the T-junction towards Cudliptown and Peter Tavy. Soon the pinnacles of Peter Tavy church come into view above t he hedge to the right. The church is to the right of the main road through the village. **Take an unsignposted turn on the left (with a Ministry of Defence notice board) when the main road bends to the right to descend to Harford Bridge. Continue up the hill to come to a crossroads and turn left to Princetown and Horrabridge. This lane, which is initially steep and overhung with trees, climbs to reach the B3357 (Tavistock to Princetown road). Turn left towards Princetown.**

The road climbs steeply to the top of Whitchurch Common. There is a car park to the right where one may pause to enjoy the magnificent view to the south and west. Vixen Tor is prominent to the south-east. **Continue along the Princetown road past the Merrivale quarries and the Dartmoor Inn to the left.** The latter is at the bottom of the valley of the River Walkham. When the road climbs again there is a car park on the right which is useful for exploring the Merrivale antiquities – an assortment of Bronze Age remains, including a remarkable stone avenue known as 'The Graveyard'.

Bear right when the road divides B by a telephone-box, following the sign to Princetown. The prison can be seen to the left as the road descends into the town. The High Moorland Visitor Centre occupies the former Duchy Hotel.

At Princetown, when you are at the T-junction faced with the Devil's Elbow pub, turn left towards Two Bridges. Then turn immediately right by an old chapel, passing the

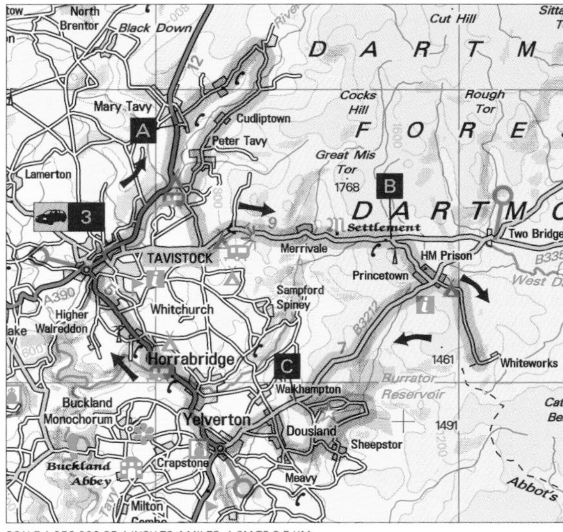

SCALE 1:250 000 OR 1 INCH TO 4 MILES *1 CM TO 2.5 KM*

Burrator Reservoir, a beautiful man-made feature of Dartmoor

Fox Tor Café car park to the right and crossing a cattle-grid. This road takes you into one of the loneliest parts of Dartmoor. The landscape is barren and there are no dramatic landscape features. Soon the road runs parallel to the Devonport Leat, built in 1793 to supply water to Devonport and Plymouth. When Burrator Reservoir was built in 1898 the leat was diverted to flow into it, thus it continued to serve its original purpose (the reservoir being the principal source of the city's water supply). The six-foot- (1.8 m) wide aqueduct takes water from a remote part of the moor and gently descends a course following the contours. At Whiteworks it flowed through a tunnel and crossed the watershed of the River Meavy. There are plenty of places to park by this road. The lonely ways which lead off into the moor from

• PLACES OF INTEREST •

Merrivale

In many ways Merrivale is the most fascinating of all historic sites on Dartmoor. Just before you reach the famous Dartmoor Inn you will see the Merrivale quarry, the last one operating on the moor. After the pub, on the banks of the little River Walkham, there is evidence of tin working, with several blowing houses (smelt houses) to the north of the road. A little further on you come to the Merrivale Antiquities, a collection of hut circles, cairns, cists, and stone avenues. They all date from the Bronze Age, apart from the large circular stones. They are half-finished millstones intended for crushing cider apples.

Princetown

The story of Princetown began in 1785. Thomas Tyrwhitt, Secretary of the Duchy of Cornwall, persuaded the Prince of Wales to set up an estate here of 2,300 acres in order to transform barren moorland into cultivated land. Unfortunately, the combination of the thin soil of the moors plus a hostile climate – Princetown is 1,430 feet (436 m) above sea-level and the highest town in England – meant that no worthwhile crops were produced. So, in 1805, he suggested building a prison on the site. His royal patron readily agreed to this, acknowledging the need to accommodate prisoners captured in the wars then being waged with France. The first French prisoners came to Dartmoor in 1808. American prisoners-of-war succeeded the French in 1812, and many died in the riots which frequently erupted – seven thousand prisoners were held in extremely cramped conditions. In 1816, at the end of the wars, the prison was closed for thirty-four years until it re-opened in 1850 as a criminal prison. The colonies had, by then, become tired of receiving ill-doers transported from Britain. Today, the prison houses just six hundred inmates, and Princetown depends on tourists to maintain its precarious prosperity.

The National Park has set up the High Moorland Visitor Centre in the former Duchy Hotel in an attempt to bring more tourists to the town.

High Moorland Visitor Centre, Princetown. The centre uses interactive computers as well as life-size figures (including Sherlock Holmes) to shed light on all aspects of life on Dartmoor, past and present. Audio visual theatre and art gallery. Open daily Easter–October 10–5. Winter 10–4. Telephone: (01822) 890414.

here are very popular with walkers. A favourite walk from a point near the end of the lane is to the Burrator Reservoir, about 3 miles to the west. The road crosses the leat to come to the handful of cottages at the end of the lane at Whiteworks.

The bogs here, like Foxton Mire below Fox Tor, are supposed to have inspired the horrendous Grimpen Mire in the *Hound of the Baskervilles*. Just below Fox Tor is Childe's Tomb. Childe was a hunter who, during the reign of Edward III, got lost in a snow storm. He killed his horse and used the carcass as a shelter but, nevertheless, died of exposure. He left a note saying that whoever buried him could have his lands. The monks of Tavistock found his body and hurried to carry out the condition of the bequest. Ghostly monks have been seen here carrying a body.

There is a more interesting skyline on the return journey and, as you near Princetown, a striking view of the prison.

Back at Princetown town centre (where there is a choice of pubs and cafés) turn left on to the B3212 towards Yelverton and Plymouth. There are wide views of the moor and a succession of tors on the skyline ahead as you drive south-westwards. There are parking places off this stretch of road for those wishing to walk or pause to enjoy the panorama. The road begins to descend, and crosses a cattle-grid as it approaches the woods surrounding Burrator reservoir. **Descend a hill and, at a crossroads, just as a second belt of trees begin, turn sharply left C off the main road.** The road climbs up on to a pleasant stretch of moor. The Scots pines and other trees give depth to the landscape. **Bear left when the road divides on to a lesser lane.** This descends through woodland and passes plenty of possible picnic places. The Devonport Leat runs alongside the lane for some distance before the road bends to the right to cross it. A stone cross stands in the bracken nearby. **The lane drops steeply to a T-junction. Turn left here and follow the lane as it crosses two streams.** This is another popular place for picnics.

One of the Merrivale standing stones with King Tor beyond

The road now follows the shore of the reservoir with woods to the right. The granite walls have ferns and flowers growing from the cracks between the huge stones. **At a T-junction turn sharply right. Follow the road across the top of the dam and then turn left at the next junction to pass toilets on the left.** After this there is a steep drop to the left protected by a line of granite posts. At the end of these there is open moorland providing views westwards to Cornwall. **Cross a cattle-grid and then bear right towards Dousland. When you meet the B3212 by the Burritor Inn turn left to reach Yelverton.** There are pubs and a café here as well as the unique Paperweight Centre – an exhibition of eight hundred antique and modern glass paperweights. **From Yelverton take the A386 to return to Tavistock.** ■

Dartmoor Prison at Princetown

• TOUR 4 •

KINGSBRIDGE, SALCOMBE AND BURGH ISLAND

44 MILES – 2 HOURS
START AND FINISH AT KINGSBRIDGE

This drive allows many fine vistas of the coastline, but the walker enjoys the best scenery. So do try to find the time to walk the short distance from the lovely garden at Sharpitor to view the Kingsbridge estuary from Bolt Head. This is one of the finest panoramas in England. The lane along the north bank of the River Avon from Aveton Gifford is delightful. However, this byway may be submerged if the tide is high and can be bypassed if necessary.

Leave Kingsbridge on the A381, heading for Salcombe. Pass through the villages of West Alvington and Malborough. About 1/2 mile after the latter village a tiny lane on the left goes to Yarde Medieval Farmhouse.

If you wish to explore Salcombe there is a convenient park-and-drive arrangement operating from this main road, just as it begins to descend into the town. Parking in Salcombe is extremely scarce. **Continue into Salcombe, turning left off Main Road to make for the town centre.** Pass the church before reaching the colourful waterfront. **Follow the one-way system past the war memorial and the Marine Hotel.**

Burgh Island was once a haunt of smugglers

Turn left down Sandhills Road which zigzags to the shore at North Sands. If you do not intend to visit Sharpitor it is advisable to fork right as you climb the hill from North Sands. The turn is marked by a wall-mounted letter-box and is signposted to Malborough. Turn left to Combe at the first major junction and rejoin the route at Combe Cross.

However, the tour continues to South Sands. Here the National Trust own the

• PLACES OF INTEREST •

Kingsbridge
There was a settlement here in Saxon times. The bridge was established in 962 to link the royal estates on each side of the river. The monks of Buckfast owned a manor at Kingsbridge and, in 1219, began a market. As the town grew the streets began to climb up the steep sides of the valley.

The church dates from the thirteenth century, though the first recorded consecration was in 1414. It was much altered in the nineteenth century. A plaque is to be found on the southern exterior wall of the chancel commemorating Robert (commonly called Bone) Phillip, who died in 1793. It reads:

Here I lie at the chancel door
Here I lie because I'm poor.
The further in the more you'll
pay
Here I lie as warm as they.

Kingsbridge has much to offer visitors today, notably its excellent shops and eating places, many of which feature locally-caught seafood. Market day is on Tuesdays.

The Cookworthy Museum of Rural Life, Fore Street. The museum occupies the Grammar School founded in 1670 and takes its name from William Cookworthy, a native of Kingsbridge. He discovered kaolin and is acclaimed as being the 'father' of English porcelain. It features reconstructions of a Victorian kitchen and an Edwardian pharmacy, as well as an extensive collection of local history items.

Open all year April–September Mondays–Saturdays 10–5. October Mondays–Fridays 10.30–4. November–March by arrangement. Telephone: (01548) 853235.

SCALE 1:166 666 OR ABOUT 1 INCH TO $2\frac{1}{2}$ MILES *1 CM TO 1.66 KM*

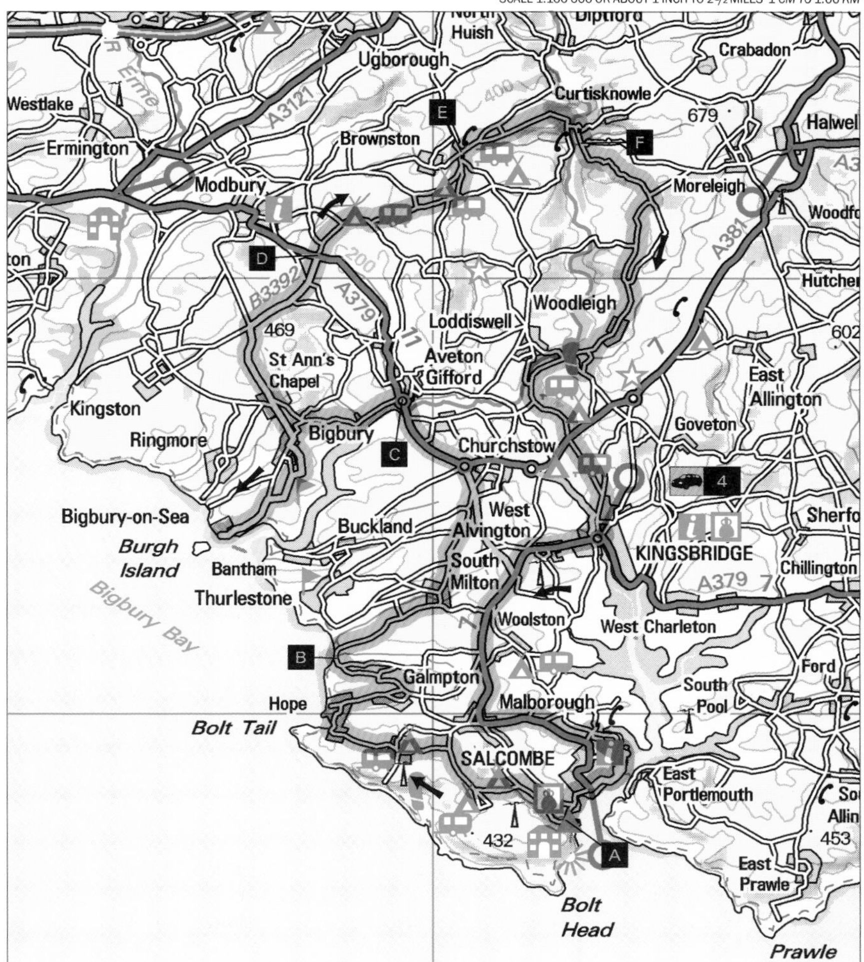

beautiful sub-tropical gardens at Sharpitor from where there are wonderful views of the coastline and estuary. The house, Overbecks, is a Youth Hostel which also accommodates a local history museum. You may park in the National Trust car park and walk along the Coastal Path to Bolt Head and beyond. **Return from the car park and bear left at the entrance to Sharpitor A to head for Malborough. Fork left at Combe Cross and then turn right at Rew Cross where you join a major road coming from Soar. Take the next turn left to Hope Cove and pass through the hamlet of Bolberry.** Inner Hope is picturesque with beautiful thatched cottages. Walks from here climb up to Bolt Tail and then strike eastwards towards Bolt Head and Salcombe.

Continue on the main road to a T-junction where you can turn left if you wish to see Outer Hope. Otherwise, turn right to Galmpton. Turn left at the end of the village on to the road to Thurlestone Sands. The National Trust has a notice, where the road becomes a track along the shore, which says that this is a 'vehicular right of way not maintained at public expense'. **This track allows access to a shoreline car park B and a route to South Milton.**

In South Milton turn left at the post office and then, after $\frac{1}{4}$ mile, turn right to follow signs to Churchstow and Modbury. Cross straight over the junctions at Upton and Huxton Crosses. Bear right at the T-junction which follows and then turn left on to the main road at Elston Cross and then left again on to the main road. Keep straight on when you come to the roundabout and follow the A379 to Aveton Gifford.

The village is reached over a bridge 1,200 feet (366 m) long, much of it dating from medieval times. Aveton Gifford's church, one of the finest in Devon, was destroyed by a random bomb in the Second World War. It was painstakingly rebuilt between 1948 and 1957 as a copy of the original. The restoration is a triumph for twentieth century craftsmen, even the roof bosses have been faithfully reproduced.

Cross the bridge and turn left C at the roundabout. There is parking to the right. **Follow the lane marked as a tidal ford. If the road is flooded, you can wait a little for the tide to retreat, or bypass the lane by continuing on the A379 to Ashford (the hamlet after Aveton Gifford) and then turn left to rejoin the route at Bigbury.**

However, the tidal road close to the river is delightful. There are a few picnic places by the river before the road begins to climb away from the shore. Gourmets will appreciate the oystery to be found here. **Turn left to Bigbury at the first junction. At Pond Green turn left towards Bigbury-on-Sea.** A golf course is to the left. Views along the coast unfold as the road descends into the small resort with its thatched cottages. If the tide is out you can

• *PLACES OF INTEREST* •

Yarde Medieval Farmhouse, near Malborough.
A property mentioned in the Domesday Book. The facade of the farmhouse dates from 1718 but behind this, surrounding a courtyard, is much older fabric. Visitors are welcome if a contribution is made towards the restoration of the farm. An ancient brewing vat as big as a swimming pool can be seen.

Open Easter–September Sundays, Wednesdays and Fridays 2–5. Telephone: (01548) 842367.

Salcombe
Salcombe's parish church accurately reflects the town's development. It dates from 1843 and was enlarged in 1889, at which time Salcombe was well on the way to becoming the boating resort we know today. Until the late eighteenth century Salcombe was a small shipbuilding village, but then members of the gentry discovered the great beauty of its estuary as well as the warmth of its climate and began building villas to make the most of the views.

Salcombe Castle, also known as Fort Charles, guards the estuary at North Sands, and was part of the coastal defences built by Henry VIII. It was the last Royalist garrison in the county to surrender, and only did so when it received assurances that the castle would thenceforward be known as Fort Charles. The Roundheads immediately slighted it.

Overbecks Museum and Garden, Sharpitor. The sub-tropical gardens provide a magnificent foreground for a panorama over Salcombe and Kingsbridge. Palms, agapanthus and mimosa flourish in the garden and its magnolias are magnificent. The museum in the Edwardian house displays photographs, documents, and artifacts illustrating the maritime history of Salcombe. There is a secret room for children.

Museum open March–October daily except Saturday 11–5.30. Garden open daily throughout the year 10–8, or sunset if earlier. Telephone: (01548)842893 or 843238.

Thurlestone
Thurleston derives its name from the old word 'thirl' meaning 'pierced with a hole'. Thurlestone Rock, just offshore, has a hole etched through it by the power of the sea. It has made a perfect rock arch, a feature mentioned in the *Domesday Book*.

This part of the coastline was particularly dangerous to sailing ships which could easily become trapped in the bay if a strong south-westerly was blowing. Their plight was not helped by the activities of locals who sometimes lured vessels on to the shore by showing false lights. They would then mercilessly plunder the wrecks. In 1772 the *Chantiloupe* went aground close to Thurlestone Rock and quickly broke up. A wealthy passenger, Mrs Burke, seeing imminent disaster, put on her finest silks and all her jewellery in the belief that this finery would ensure her being rescued from the surf. The wreckers certainly noticed her – they pulled her, unconscious, out of the sea, and then proceeded to hack off her fingers to remove the rings she wore. Mrs Burke subsequently died, though not before cursing those who speeded her demise. All three wreckers suffered painful deaths before the year was out!

Burgh Island
The islet was once surmounted by a small chapel dedicated to St Michael, an echo of more famous offshore islands in Mounts Bay and in Normandy. The chapel later became a huer's house, where a watchman scanned the water for signs of pilchard shoals. This industry is reflected in the name of the island's famous pub. The hotel (now made into apartments) was built in 1929 as a casino, and was meant to rival that at Monte Carlo. It attracted many famous guests, amongst them Agatha Christie. She was inspired to write *Ten Little Niggers* (now retitled *And Then There Were None*) and *Evil under the Sun* while staying here.

An earlier resident of Burgh Island was Tom Crocker, a famous pirate who made it his headquarters. Crocker was brought to justice and hung in 1395. His ghost is supposed to walk here, appearing during the third week of August each year, ignoring the celebrations arranged at this time in his memory.

Sorley Tunnel Leisure Farm
Provides educational and leisure activities on a working farm. Model railway and craft workshops. Open daily April–October 10.30–6. Telephone: (01548) 857711 or 854078.

A view of Hope Cove, near Salcombe

walk across the sand to Burgh Island, otherwise you can use the sea tractor service.

The road to Bigbury-on-Sea is a cul-de-sac and you have to return to Bigbury village. From here continue along the B3392 to reach the A379 at Harraton Cross D. Cross straight over here heading for a road signposted to Pennymore and Southleigh Caravan Parks. Bear right at Treheale Cross to pass a caravan park and then follow the main road at Heathfield Cross towards Loddiswell. Pass a second caravan park. A pleasant stretch through woodland follows. **Keep on the main road towards South Brent. When you come to the main road bear right towards a garage and then turn right E after this (opposite the California Inn) following the sign to Moreleigh, Halwell and Dartmouth.**

The road runs along the side of a lovely valley and into woods. It crosses the River Avon over Gara Bridge, built for pack-horses but later widened. **Take the first turning to the right F after the bridge on to an unsign-posted road running along the edge of a wood.** This quiet lane climbs steeply. **Be careful as, at one point, a right-hand corner comes on you unexpectedly when a misleading track goes straight ahead. At Preston Cross keep straight on to join a main road. Bear right at Preston Fork.** The road twists round Preston Farm and then passes Wotton Farm to reach Woodleigh.

From Woodleigh the road descends into the valley and goes beneath an old railway bridge to pass the Avon Mill Garden Centre where there is a tearoom. **When you reach the main road at Rake Corner the route continues to the left towards Kingsbridge.** Pass the entrance to Sorley Tunnel on the right where there are craft workshops, a farm centre and a tearoom. **Cross straight over the B3194 to return to Kingsbridge.** ■

Kingsbridge is a popular boating centre

• TOUR 5 •

TAVISTOCK, LYDFORD GORGE AND BUCKLAND ABBEY

40 MILES – 2 HOURS
START AND FINISH AT TAVISTOCK

Early in this drive Brent Tor and Lydford Gorge offer romantic scenery. Later, there is much of historical interest. Morwellham Quay is one of the finest of our living museums, illustrating industrial and social history. Another reminder of the past is Buckland Abbey, a beautiful house which was once the home of Sir Francis Drake. The end of the route takes you to a hidden beauty spot by the lovely River Walkham, a delightful surprise to end the tour.

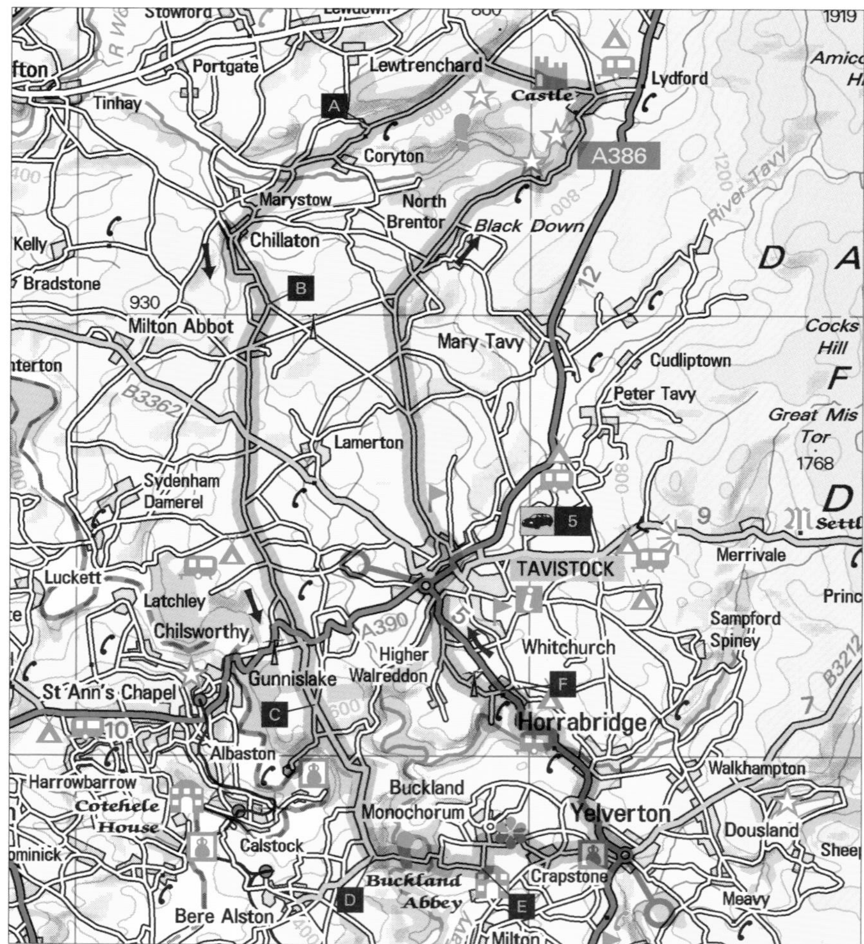

SCALE 1:166 666 OR ABOUT 1 INCH TO 2½ MILES *1 CM TO 1.66 KM*

From Bedford Square, in the centre of Tavistock, take Drake Road, between the Midland Bank on the right and Lloyds Bank to the left. Climb the hill and pass under the viaduct. After leaving the town Brent Tor is clearly seen ahead crowned by its church. The road runs northwards in a very straight line. **A turn to Lifton and Chillaton leaves to the left, and one to Mary Tavy to the right.** There are wide views to the right when the hedges allow. As the road nears Brent Tor it forms the western edge of the National Park. There is a car park to the left of the road (with toilets) for those wishing to undertake the short, but steep, climb to the church which crowns the conical hill.

The village of North Brentor is off to the right. Shortly after this the road reaches the lower car park for visitors to Lydford Gorge (this is the waterfall entrance). **After the Mucky Duck Inn the road crosses a bridge over the long-disused railway and so comes to Lydford itself.** The upper, main entrance to the gorge is just before the bridge across the river. After this the road climbs to reach the village passing first the church and then the castle. The main street has pubs and a tea shop.

Buckland Abbey, the home of Sir Francis Drake

Turn left at the war memorial to Coryton. Keep on the main road. Pass an entrance to Lydford Wood on the left where there is a car park and forest trail. After this the road narrows, and there is soon woodland to the right. **Bear left A to Coryton church when a road leaves to the right to Lewdown.** There are now fine views to the right, although you may have to pause at a gateway to enjoy them! Coryton church is down a small lane to the left of this road – the churchyard gives wonderful views. **Turn left when you reach the main road and head for Tavistock.**

After Chillaton the road runs above a wooded gorge and climbs steadily. **At the top of the hill take the turn to the right B signposted to Lamerton and Milton Abbot. Take this road and cross the B3362.** Continue on the straight road going through rich farmland. The hamlet of Chipshop must be mis-named – it has no chip shop! After the road crosses the A390 it becomes the B3257, heading for Bere Alston

• *PLACES OF INTEREST* •

Brent Tor

Brent Tor is the most easily recognised Dartmoor landmark, a place of stark beauty. The tor is the weathered remains of an ancient volcano. At 1,130 feet (344 m) it provides a magnificent viewpoint over Dartmoor, the coastline of south Devon, and much of Cornwall. The tor itself provided the building stone for the tiny church dedicated to St Michael. It dates from c. 1140 and was built by Robert Giffard at his own expense. It was rebuilt in the following century when it belonged to Tavistock Abbey. Henry III authorised a three-day fair to take place here to celebrate St Michael's feast-day.

Few today would disagree with the description by Tristram Risdon, written in 1630:

...a church full bleak and weather beaten, all alone, as it were forsaken, whose church yard doth hardly afford depth of earth to bury the dead; yet doubtless they rest there as securely as in sumptuous St Peter's, until the day of doom.

Lydford Gorge

Risdon also commented on Lydford Gorge, saying that 'it may be numbered amongst the wonders of this kingdom'. In the eighteenth century its dramatic cascades appealed to the fashionable notions of picturesque, natural landscape.

Tourists, including many artists, were attracted to Lydford. Famous watercolourists, like Thomas Girtin and Richard Wilson, found the gorge to be a popular subject with their patrons, and writers, such as Charles Kingsley, also used its wild beauty as a setting.

It is a notable habitat of woodpeckers, bats and woodland butterflies. The foliage is at its best in the spring (also when the bluebells are out) and in autumn. The National Trust warn that the paths may be slippery at all seasons and that some visitors may find them arduous. Only the waterfall entrance is open in the winter. The path downstream is closed beyond the foot of the White Lady Waterfall.

Open April–October daily 10–5.30. November–March daily 10.30–3 (see above). Telephone: (0182282) 441 or 320.

and Morwellham Quay.

If you wish to visit the famous living museum, turn right after about a mile C down the road to Morwellham, otherwise remain on the B3257.

About 3 miles south from here, just before Bere Alston and at a point where the main road swings to the right, make an acute turn left D on to the road to Buckland Monachorum. The narrow road descends steeply down a gradient of 1-in-4, through woods which seem about to smother the lane. **Cross a bridge over the River**

• PLACES OF INTEREST •

Lydford village

Lydford, with its beautiful church and forbidding castle, is a delightful place. Few people would suspect that a thousand years ago, until medieval times, it was one of the most important towns in the west of England. It came to prominence as one of Alfred the Great's main centres of administration. It had its own mint and was defended by a massive rampart of earth topped with a stockade. The present stone castle dates from 1195. It was built as a prison to hold those who transgressed Dartmoor's strict hunting and stannary laws.

In the churchyard look for the gravestone of George Routledge, the village watchmaker, who died in 1802. Its inscription pursues the allegory of his blameless life with the craft he followed:

Integrity was the mainspring
And prudence the regulator
Of all the actions of his life...

and so on at great length.

Morwellham Quay

In the 1850s the copper mines of west Devon and Cornwall supplied more than half of the world's demand for copper. The Devon Great Consols Mine at Blanchdown, just upstream of Morwellham, was a particularly

rich source for the mineral, and employed eleven hundred men. There were other mines on Dartmoor, and production at Wheal Friendship near Mary Tavy in the late eighteenth century created the need for better transport links. Thus, a canal was constructed from Tavistock to the River Tamar at Morwellham Quay. The barges were then lowered 250 feet (76 m) on trolleys down an inclined plane to be unloaded into waiting ships. This remarkable procedure is explained in the living museum at Morwellham which not only sheds light on the mining industry of the region, but examines many other aspects of its life in former ages. Guides and workpeople wear costumes of the 1860s. Children, as well as adults, can spend a day at Morwellham exploring the varied attractions. There is even a Victorian schoolroom in the charge of a schoolmaster employing the strict discipline of the era.

Open all year (though operations are reduced in winter). Summer 10–5.30 (last admission 3.30). Winter 10–4.30 (last admission 2.30). Telephone: (01822) 832766.

Buckland Abbey

The abbey was founded in 1278. The first abbot was a Cistercian monk from Quarr Abbey on the Isle of Wight. The Cistercians were great farmers and, by the end of the fourteenth century, their estate at Buckland covered twenty thousand acres.

When the monastery was dissolved in 1541 its buildings were bought by Sir Richard Grenville. His grandson, another Sir Richard Grenville (he later won fame for his heroism aboard the *Revenge*) converted the abbey church into a mansion in 1576. He built three floors into the soaring height of its nave and placed a tower where the crossing was originally situated. This was where Grenville built his Great Hall, concealing its medieval origins and decorating it with flamboyant Tudor plasterwork. Elsewhere many details of the original monastery survive, in spite of damage caused by a serious fire in 1938.

In 1581 Grenville sold the property to Sir Francis Drake and, though Drake died without issue, it remained in his family until 1946. In 1948 the abbey was given to the National Trust who, aided by the Pilgrim Trust, arranged for it to be run by the City of Plymouth as a museum, with exhibits placing particular emphasis on the exploits of Sir Francis Drake. The abbey's fifteenth-century tithe barn, a splendid structure 154 feet (47 m) long, stands next to the house, a reminder of the prosperity the monastery enjoyed.

Open April–October daily except Thursdays 10.30–5.30. November–March Saturdays and Sundays 2–5. Telephone: (01822) 853607.

The Garden House, east of Buckland Monachorum.

This is one of the foremost gardens to be created in the West Country in the last fifty years. It was begun in 1945. The nucleus is a two-acre walled garden. It has expanded over the years so that it now covers eight acres and contains six thousand different varieties of plants, many of them unusual.

Open March–October daily 10.30–5. Telephone: (01822) 854769.

Yelverton Paperweight Centre, Leg o' Mutton Pub, Yelverton.

The largest private collection of paperweights in Europe with more than eight hundred colourful examples. Open two weeks before Easter–October Monday–Saturday 10–5. Telephone: (01822) 854250.

Tavy and turn right. This is a very pleasant beauty spot and there are several parking places nearby. However, if you clamber over the rocks take care as these are very slippery.

Climb the steep lane up from the bridge to the T-junction E. If you wish to visit Buckland Abbey turn right. **Otherwise, to continue the route, turn left to Buckland Monachorum. Turn right into the village.** Pass a lane to the left leading to the church and pub. The church is enormous, with the vaulting in the south aisle a particular delight. Although the church was built c. 1490 this aisle was added about a century later, and the vault may have been adapted from that of Buckland Abbey. It rises above a magnificent monument to General Elliott, later Lord Heathfield, who valiantly defended Gibraltar against the Spaniards between 1779 and 1783. The marble plaques show the course of the siege in fascinating detail, including men heating cannon balls. The explanation for this is that the Spanish had mounted their guns on rafts and Elliott thwarted their bombardment by means of red-hot cannon balls which set the rafts on fire. The General married into the Drake family, and there are several other Drake monuments in this aisle, though none are direct descendants of Sir Francis who died childless. However, many people visit the church to see the pew supposed to have been used by Admiral Drake. It is behind the font and has a carving of the *Golden Hinde* above a representation of the globe.

The route continues through the village, without diverting to the church, and soon reaches the Garden House on the eastern edge of the village. This is one of the West Country's most celebrated gardens. **Continue on this road to pass through Crapstone and reach a large common. Take the turning left signposted to Yelverton. Cross the common to meet the A386 at Yelverton. Turn left here towards Tavistock. At the roundabout take the first exit to stay on the A386.** Pass the Paperweight Centre and the pub on the left.

Dartmoor's most famous landmark – Brent Tor

Go past turnings to the right to Horrabridge and cross the River Walkham over Bedford Bridge. The road climbs through woods into Grenofen. **Just before the Halfway House Inn turn left F. Turn left again after 1/4 mile.** Descend a steep hill and cross an extremely narrow bridge to reach a delightful picnic place on the banks of the River Walkham. From here you can walk along the bank of the river to Double Waters, a remote beauty spot where the Walkham joins the Tavy.

Climb the hill back from the bridge and turn left at the top to pass a radio mast. Go straight over a crossroads. At a T-junction turn right to pass through an industrial estate and rejoin the A386 on the outskirts of Tavistock. ■

Beautiful Lydford Gorge

• TOUR 6 •

TOTNES, DITTISHAM AND BRENT MOOR

40 MILES – 2 HOURS
START AND FINISH AT TOTNES

There could hardly be more variety in a drive than that offered by this route. It begins by winding past a series of creeks leading off the lovely River Dart and through the beautiful villages of Tuckenhay and Dittisham. After this it heads inland through South Brent and then climbs to Shipley Bridge, a moorland beauty spot from where there is an easy walk to the Avon Reservoir. The return is via Buckfastleigh and Dartington.

Take the A381 southwards out of Totnes, heading for Kingsbridge. There are good views of the town as you climb the hill. **Be careful not to miss the turn to the left A signposted to Ashprington, Tuckenhay, Cornworthy and Bow Bridge.** After about 1/4 mile you will pass the entrance to Bowden House. Its Queen Anne facade masks fabric of a Tudor house. It has a splendid reception room lavishly decorated in baroque style. The house is open to the public.

Fore Street in Totnes is lined with countless interesting old buildings

Keep on the main road into Ashprington. This is a very attractive village. The church with its slim, tapering tower is to the left. It underwent comprehensive nineteenth-century restoration. **Bear right at the war memorial to pass the post office and descend a steep hill. At the T-junction at Bow Bridge turn left to Tuckenhay and Cornworthy.** The road follows the southern side of Bow Creek to reach Tuckenhay, picturesquely situated on an inlet off the creek.

This was a busy little port in the nineteenth century, with ships loading road stone at the quays and bringing wood pulp to the two paper-mills, one of which has a clock tower. Tuckenhay takes its name from Abraham Tucker who built the quays and warehouses in 1806. The paper-mills, originally built as woollen-mills, are now holiday apartments.

The road passes Floyd's Inn and the former paper-mills at the end of the village. **Follow the main road round to the left when a lane leaves to the right to Washbourne. At Cornworthy Cross keep on towards Dittisham. Almost immediately you come to Abbey Cross B where you are faced with the remains of an old abbey gatehouse.** This belonged to a small Augustinian nunnery, and dates from c. 1400. **Turn right here to East Cornworthy and go straight over crossroads at Furze Hill and Longland Crosses to reach East Cornworthy.** You will enjoy spectacular views of the river as the road descends.

Continue through East Cornworthy. The very narrow, twisting lane crosses a little bridge to come into Dittisham, a famous beauty spot once noted for its plum orchards. Before the head of a small creek, look out for the old millrace to the left of the road. The church faces you

SCALE 1:250 000 OR 1 INCH TO 4 MILES *1 CM TO 2.5 KM*

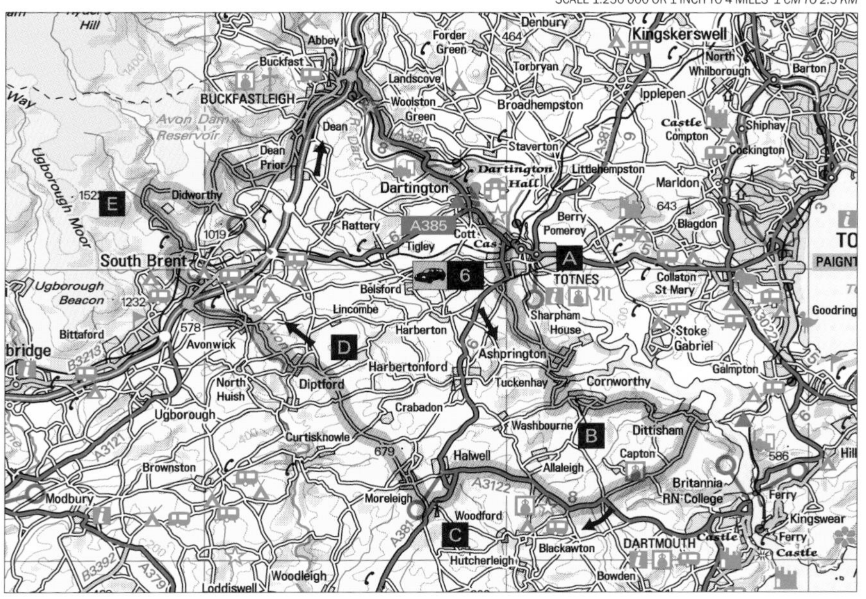

• *PLACES OF INTEREST* •

Totnes
This is as delightful a country town as any to be found in England, full of interesting and beautiful buildings. It was established as a royal town in Saxon times. However, its importance increased with the coming of the Normans when it was granted to Judhael of Brittany, one of King William's most trusted lieutenants.
He excavated the steep-sided motte making it 50 feet (15 m) high to overawe the townspeople and placed a horseshoe-shaped bailey around it. Judhael fell from royal favour when he was found to be plotting against the monarch. His successors strengthened the defence works with a fine stone keep with walls 6 feet (1.8 m) thick.

In medieval times the town prospered as a market centre – it was sited at the highest navigable point on the River Dart and also where the lowest bridge was situated. Trade in woollens helped finance the rebuilding of the large church in the fifteenth century. Its beautiful stone screen dates from this time, attempting to rival the one in the Lady Chapel of Exeter Cathedral. Traces of paint and gilding remain to remind us of its former magnificence. The fortunes of the Totnes merchants seem to have peaked in Tudor times, and sixty-six of its houses date from before 1700. The best of them are to be seen in Fore Street and High Street. The Buttermarket has an outstanding sequence of houses with upper floors projecting over the pavement. Many have rooms with magnificent plasterwork as do rooms at the Totnes Museum in Fore Street. This is a four-storey house dating from 1575. It displays many of the most idiosyncratic period features demanded by a wealthy citizen at that time.

Totnes Museum, 70 Fore Street. The house is fascinating in itself, but also contains interesting exhibits. One room is devoted to Charles Babbage, credited with inventing the forerunner of the computer. Open Easter–October Mondays–Fridays and Bank Holidays 10.30–1, 2–5. Telephone: (01803) 863821.

Totnes Motor Museum, Steamer Quay. Private collection of vintage sports and racing cars spanning eighty years of motoring. Open daily Easter–October 10–5. Telephone: (01803) 862777.

Totnes Castle. The best example of a motte-and-bailey castle in Devon. Open all year

April–September daily 10–6. October–March Wednesday–Sunday 10–4. Telephone: (01803) 864406.

Bowden House. The house incorporates a mansion built in 1510 for John Giles, reputedly the wealthiest man in Devon at the time. It was remodelled in 1704 when the Queen Anne facade was added and the baroque Great Hall built. It is also the home of the British Photographic Museum which has unique cameras illustrating the history of photography and the cinema.

British Photographic Museum. Open mid-March–mid-October Monday–Thursday and Bank Holiday Sundays, from noon. Telephone: (01803) 863664.

as you enter Dittisham. The unusual pulpit in the church is of painted stone with naively-carved figures standing in canopied niches. The building dates from 1333 though the pulpit, and much else, is fifteenth-century work. A passenger ferry connects Dittisham with Churston and Torbay.

The road swings round to the right to pass a pub. A road to the left, just past the church, leads down to a car park by the river. **Follow the signs to Dartmouth and Totnes out of the village up a very steep hill (1-in-5).** Pass a turning to Kingston on the right. The next turn right goes to Capton. A sign points down this lane to a prehistoric hill settlement museum, farm shop and winery. **Keep to the main road to come to the A3122 at the Sportsman's Arms pub and turn right.** Pass Dartmouth Golf and Country Club on the right and then Woodlands Leisure Park to the left (an attraction certain to appeal to children).

After 2½ miles turn left at Totnes Cross on to the A381 to head towards Kingsbridge. At the top of the hill turn right C on to a lane signposted to Moreleigh and Modbury. At Moreleigh take the turn right to Diptford opposite the post office. However, if you wish to visit Moreleigh church, keep on through the village.

This narrow lane may prove to be unexpectedly busy so watch out for passing places. The rich pasture-land here is typical of inland Devon. **Pass Crabadon and then Combeshead Crosses, keeping on the main road. At Christone Cross D bear left off the main road following the sign to Diptford and Avonwick.** As the road drops into Diptford there is a pleasant view of a patchwork of small fields with the hills of Dartmoor beyond. **Bear left on**

• *PLACES OF INTEREST* •

Capton Hill Settlement Museum
A Stone Age site dating back at least eight thousand years. Reconstructed round house and collection of artefacts. Farm walk. Open March–October daily 10–5. Telephone: (01803) 712452.

Moreleigh Church
In 1270 the vicar of Woodleigh fell out with a local squire, Sir Peter de Fishacre of Moreleigh. Sir Peter was a mean and ill-tempered knight and, in a fit of rage, decapitated the priest who opposed him. Even a Norman knight could not get away with this sort of behaviour, and Sir Peter was ordered to build a new church as retribution. He did so at Moreleigh. It is said that when he died he was not allowed to be buried in his church and a special extension on the south side had to be built to accommodate his tomb.

Buckfast Butterfly Farm and Otter Sanctuary
A unique attraction which combines a tropical forest, where you may see exotic butterflies, with an outdoor aquatic park, designed to display the fun-loving otters to best advantage. There is a special viewing tunnel underneath one of the pools, and a system of mirrors allowing you to look inside a holt without disturbing its residents. Otter Sanctuary open March– November daily 10–5.30 or dusk. Buckfast Butterflies open late March–early November daily 10–5.30 or dusk. Telephone: (01364) 642916.

South Devon Railway
A seven-mile-long preserved steam railway which runs by the side of the River Dart from Buckfastleigh to the outskirts of Totnes. Services run daily during the Easter week and late May Bank Holiday– September. Wednesdays, Saturdays and Sundays April, May and October. Telephone: (01364) 42338.

Buckfastleigh
The town has always suffered from being situated close to Ashburton which, as a stannary town, had an immediate advantage. Nevertheless, Buckfastleigh enjoyed a golden era in the late eighteenth and early nineteenth centuries when several woollen mills were established.

The ruins of the parish church are sited on a hilltop to the north of the town. In the churchyard is the tomb of Richard Capel; described as a 'penthouse' tomb it looks more like a prison. Perhaps it needs to be, for Capel, who died in 1677, was a very nasty local squire who forced his attentions on most of the young women in the neighbourhood. As he lay on his deathbed the hell-hounds howled around the house, waiting to escort his soul to the Devil. Local children dare one another to walk round his tomb thirteen times and then poke a finger through the keyhole. Few take up the challenge, believing that Capel will gnaw off the finger. On a night in early July Capel's headless ghost, with a pack of whisht hounds, rides up the drive of his home, Brook Manor, 2 miles to the west of the town. The evil squire is supposed to have inspired Sir Arthur Conan Doyle with the character of Black Hugo in *Hound of the Baskervilles*.

Pennywell Farm. The Farm and Wildlife Centre is one of Devon's foremost animal attractions. It incorporates a Falconry Centre. Open April–October daily 10–5.30. Telephone: (01364) 642023.

Dartington Cider Press Centre
The unique retail and exhibition centre shows some of the country's leading craft work, including Dartington crystal. Craftsmen are often in attendance to demonstrate their skills. Open daily all year, Mondays–Saturdays 9.30–5.30. Telephone: (01803) 864171.

There is a fine walk to the Avon Reservoir from Shipley Bridge

to a main road and follow this through the village towards Avonwick. Diptford church has a medieval spire, a rarity in Devon. After this the road descends very steeply into the valley to run close to the river. Railway enthusiasts will spot an old station to the left of the road, its platform still intact. Signal-post tops decorate the gate-posts of the property.

Turn left at the T-junction on to the B3210 to head towards South Brent and cross the River Avon. After 1 mile you will pass the Mill Inn and then meet the main road into South Brent. Turn right to go beneath the A38. Follow the road into the village centre and turn left into the main street. Ignore the sign to Didworthy and the Avon Dam which points to the right down Station Road. Instead, go down the one-way street ahead (Church Street). This takes you past St Petrock's Church with its squat Norman tower. **Go over a railway bridge and then go straight on past the village hall on a road with a weight restriction.** A road to Lutton goes off to the right at Oakhill Cross. **Carry on towards Aish, Zeal and Didworthy and cross the tiny Lydia Bridge.** Look right to see the waterfall which becomes a raging torrent after heavy rain.

The narrow lane climbs up steeply between high banks. **Keep straight on over crossroads passing a little cluster of houses, the hamlet of Aish.** The lane climbs relentlessly. There is a deep valley to the right, well wooded and particularly beautiful in autumn.

At Shipley Bridge there is a car park for people who wish to walk on the moor. One popular route is to follow the River Avon up to the Avon Dam, a distance of about 2 miles. It is a lovely route with Shipley and Black tors overlooking the infant river. The reservoir supplies much of South Devon with water at a rate of more than two million gallons a day.

Cross Shipley Bridge E and a second cattle-grid. When you reach a junction keep ahead on the main road. Turn left at Gingaford Cross to Gidley and Skerraton. The road climbs steadily to more open country. There is a fantastic view and plenty of places to picnic before the road drops once more to cross Gidley Bridge. **Turn right at the road junction which follows. Fork right at the next turn, away from the lane going to Addislade. At Moors Head Cross go straight on towards Dean. The lane joins the South Brent to Buckfastleigh road at Clammpits Stile. Bear left to head for Dean and Buckfastleigh.** There are good views over the Dart valley. At Dean Prior there is a working forge. A road to the right goes under the A38 to Pennywell Farm and Wildlife Centre and to Dean Prior church. The poet, Robert Herrick, was vicar here for twenty years from 1654.

The main road bypasses Buckfastleigh, so divert left if you wish to visit this small town.

A bridge takes the road over the little River Mardle. The Butterfly and Otter Sanctuary is to the right. On the right you will also find the station for the South Devon Railway. You can take a steam train back to the outskirts of Totnes from here. **Carry on along the main road. Turn right to cross the A38, and take the A384 to Totnes to pass the Dart Bridge Inn. Pass Charlie's Cross where the Staverton road leaves to the left, and come to the single-track Riverford Bridge controlled by traffic lights.**

After this the road passes the church at Dartington, the drive to the hall, and the Cider Press Craft Centre, all to the left. **Bear left at the roundabout to return to Totnes.** ■

The River Dart at Dittisham

• TOUR 7 •

NEWTON ABBOT, HAYTOR ROCKS AND HAMEL DOWN

42 MILES – 2 HOURS
START AND FINISH AT NEWTON ABBOT

This route takes you through some of the finest scenery of southern Dartmoor and visits beauty spots such as Becka Falls, Haytor Rocks and New Bridge. There are plenty of places where you can stop and walk across the moor or, perhaps, climb to the top of one of the lesser-known tors to find true solitude.

Take the A383 out of Newton Abbot towards Ashburton. A road goes to Exeter to the right. Pass this and take the next turn right, signposted to Sigford and Widecombe in the Moor to cross the A38. Immediately after a bridge turn right again A to Widecombe. The narrow lane climbs steadily. After Hook Cross, where a lane leaves to Sigford, there is attractive woodland and, when the trees thin out, there are fine views to the right. **At the next cross-roads (there is another turn to Sigford to the right) keep straight on towards Widecombe.** Rippon Tor and Bag Tor can be seen to the right. **Keep to the main road and cross a cattle-grid by a group of Scots pines.** A short way beyond this there is a lovely picnic place by a little bridge.

At Cold East Cross turn right B towards Haytor and Widecombe. This lonely stretch of road, with Blackslade Mire to the left and Rippon Tor to the right, is said to be haunted by a phantom horseman. **Join the B3387 at Hemsworthy Gate and bear right towards Haytor and Bovey Tracey.**

• PLACES OF INTEREST •

Newton Abbot

The railway transformed Newton Abbot from a quiet country market town into a prosperous Victorian borough where industry (in the form of the GWR's carriage works) blended with commerce and agriculture. Fine villas were built to overlook the River Lemon, and the railway company constructed terraces of brick houses for its employees close to their workplace. The Victorians also erected commercial and public buildings in the town centre, though the demands of modern traffic have lead to the removal of many of these. All that remains of the medieval St Leonard's Church is its tower, which was left standing when the rest was demolished in the nineteenth century. It now stands as the town's centre-piece. A new church was built close by in 1835. Newton Abbot has two other medieval churches – St Mary's at Wolborough on the south side of the town, and All Saints at High Week. They illustrate the medieval development of the town which grew up as two settlements: Newton Abbot (founded by the monks of Torre Abbey c. 1196) to the south within the parish of Wolborough, and Newton Bushel to the north on the opposite side of the River Lemon. The settlements belonged to different manors. Bradley Manor survives with many of its medieval features intact, including some interior decoration. Another church of interest is St Luke's at Milber on the eastern side of the town. This is the so-called 'Dream Church'. Its unique plan, with three naves meeting before the altar, came to the vicar in a dream in 1931 (though the building was only completed in 1963). The vicar was J. Keble Martin, who became famous as the author of *British Flora*. His brother, Arthur, was the architect.

Bradley Manor (on the A381 just south of the town). The manor mainly dates from the early fifteenth century, though there is some earlier fabric. Few houses better illustrate the way of life in late medieval times. Set in seventy acres of woodland, it is a tenanted National Trust property. Open April–September Wednesdays and occasional Thursdays 2–5. Telephone: (01626)54513.

Tuckers Maltings, Teign Road. The only working malt-house open to the public where you can see the twelve stages in the process and taste the end product (as well as smell its aroma). Open Easter–October Sunday–Friday 10–4. Telephone: (01626) 334734.

SCALE 1:166 666 OR ABOUT 1 INCH TO 2½ MILES *1 CM TO 1.66 KM*

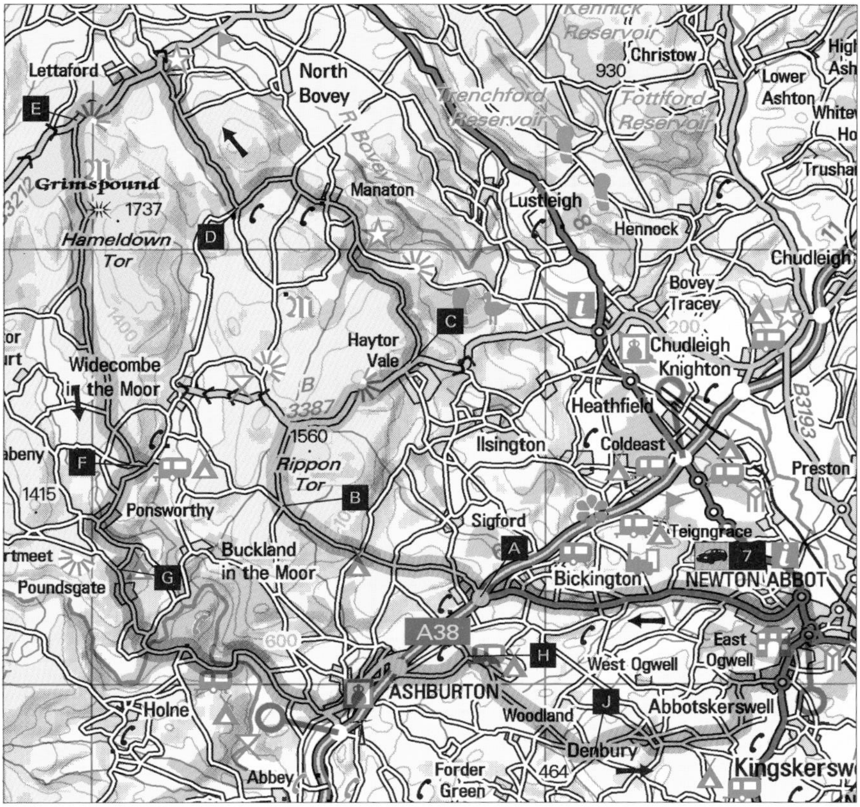

Haytor Rocks soon appear ahead and, as you climb up towards them, the view gets more spectacular until you can see the sea and the Teign estuary.

The first of the tors reached is Saddle Tor, an appetiser for the more impressive Haytor Rocks which follow. There is a choice of parking places along this stretch of road, but if you wait for the final one, just before the road to Haytor Vale, you will have a more energetic climb to the rocks themselves. An interesting feature of this part of Dartmoor is the granite tramway. This used to take stone from the quarries below Haytor down to the sea. The track bed makes an excellent footpath, and is used by the Templer Way. This was named after George Templer who made the tramway in the early nineteenth century.

Continue past the road to the right which goes to Haytor Vale. Almost immediately after this look for an unsignposted lane on the left C. Take this byway which leads across open moor towards Manaton. This is one of the most rewarding roads in Dartmoor. It has endless beautiful picnic places and footpaths into Yarner Wood to the right and up to Hound Tor on the left. **When the road leaves the moor it descends steeply to meet the Bovey Tracey to Manaton road. Turn right here if you wish to visit Becka Falls – the car park is 200 yards (183 m) along the road. Otherwise, turn left to reach Manaton.** Manaton church, which faces a

The fifteenth-century pack-horse bridge spans the River Dart at New Bridge

• PLACES OF INTEREST •

Yarner Wood
A National Nature Reserve where research is carried out into woodland management. Two woodland walks are marked out explaining the research. The wood is noted for its bilberries and for its variety of birds which include pied flycatchers and wood warblers.

Becka Falls
Like any waterfall, these cascades are seen at their best after a couple of days of rain. The main fall drops 70 feet (21 m) to a pool with moss-covered boulders. The Becka Brook then rushes through a steep, richly-wooded valley to join with the River Bovey. Public footpaths lead through the beauty spot, but the only parking nearby is in the adjacent official car park which is open Easter–October 10–6 or dusk.

River Dart Country Park
Situated by a beautiful stretch of the River Dart. The adventure playground for children is combined with woodland walks and nature trails. There are many opportunities for children to get wet on rafts, ropes or slides. Open daily Easter–September 10–5. Telephone: (01364) 52511.

lovely green, is to the right. There is a car park for those who wish to explore the countryside surrounding the village. It is possible to walk from here to Becka Falls. **Keep on through the village and turn left when a road goes off to the right to North Bovey.**

Turn right D at Heatree Cross towards Moretonhampstead. The road passes below Whooping Rock and Easdon Tor to the right. It then meanders between high hedges and stone walls. There are numerous passing places, but care is needed on this stretch.

When you reach the B3212 turn left. (The Miniature Pony Centre is ½ mile to the right.) Continue along the main road over a cattle-grid. A parking place follows to the right and is a fine viewpoint. **After this, look carefully for a road to the left E signposted to Widecombe. This is just before the road dips down into a hollow and then makes a sharp right-hand bend.**

This road climbs and suddenly a wonderful panorama is revealed southwards over Challacombe and Hamel Downs. Headland Warren is the thatched farm at the bottom of the valley to the right. Rabbits were a vital source of protein in medieval times, and the name of this farm, and the Warren House Inn on the main road, are reminders that the bleak grassland of the moor offered an ideal habitat for them.

The footpath to Grimspound goes off to the left, just before the drive to the farm meets the road. This Bronze Age settlement is situated in a saddle below Hameldown Tor, a defensive rampart protecting a large group of hut circles. The footpath up the hillside follows the course of the stream to reach one of the most interesting prehistoric sites on Dartmoor. There is a small roadside parking place. From Grimspound you can follow the Two Moors Way to reach Widecombe – a fine ridge walk.

The road gradually descends from the moorland to a more pastoral landscape. **Keep on the major road when a lane goes off to the right.** There are still fine views ahead as the road twists and turns towards Widecombe. A road from Postbridge joins from the right and, after this, the lane is enclosed and runs between high banks. However, there are still wonderful views to the right. **Pass another road to the right which goes to Broadaford and Cator.** After this the way is across open moorland again where plenty of picnic places can be found. **The road descends to a T-junction where you turn right F to Ponsworthy.** This lane is very narrow and drops down to Ponsworthy bridge where you pass the post office

The granite tramway at Haytor

Becka Falls is a famous beauty spot where you may catch sight of a kingfisher

before crossing the tiny bridge. **Continue up past lovely cottages to the road junction at Fordabridge. Keep on the main road signposted to Dartmeet and Ashburton. Bear right and keep on the main road when the way divides.** Leusdon church is on the lane to the left. The megalith, which stands on the triangle of grass just beyond the fork, commemorates the Queen's Silver Jubilee. **Turn left G at Parklandheadcross towards Poundsgate and Ashburton.** There is a fine view as the road descends a 1-in-4 gradient into Poundsgate where there is a pub and tea room.

After Poundsgate there is a short stretch of open moorland. There are picnic places to the right before the road descends steeply once more to come to New Bridge. This is a popular beauty spot with riverside walks which pass through Holne Woods. There is a car park with toilets and a National Park Information Centre.

Continue towards Ashburton. Take care – this is a busy road and there is a sheer drop to the left protected only by latticed railings. The road crosses the river again at Holne Bridge. The activities offered by the River Dart Country Park will appeal to children. After this the road descends steadily to Ashburton.

Bear left into the town centre (away from the A38). Follow the main road through the town. Pass the church and then a road to the left (North Street) which goes up to the town hall. At the end of the town turn right to cross the A38. Take the second turning on the left (not counting the spur road coming from the main road) along an unsignposted lane. This byway twists and turns as it climbs steeply. **At Combe Cross turn right H to Woodland and Denbury. Pass a turn to Woodland on the right and then the Rising Sun Tea Rooms on the left. Turn left J to Denbury at Bramble Oak. At Denbury turn right when faced by a rather strange pyramid-shaped war memorial.** This was once the water conduit for the village and bears the date 1771.

This route takes you past a road leading to a prison and into East Ogwell. **Keep on the main road passing Ogwell Green.** There is a fine view to the left here with a conveniently-placed seat. **The road drops down to a roundabout on the A381. Turn left to return to Newton Abbot.** Pass the driveway to Bradley Manor on the left and the picturesque, nineteenth-century Mackrell almshouses to reach the town centre. ■

The medieval tower of St Leonard's Church stands at the centre of Newton Abbot

• TOUR 8 •

TORQUAY, BERRY HEAD AND BERRY POMEROY

44 MILES – 2 HOURS
START AND FINISH AT TORQUAY

The route visits many of the famous places near Torbay. The two historic castles at Compton and Berry Pomeroy are highlights of the tour. It also visits a succession of villages, some famous like Stoke Gabriel and Cockington, others less well known, but hardly less appealing, which were established well before Torquay came into existence.

Follow the road along the seafront (A3022) from Torquay into Paignton. Bear left here on to the seafront road to pass the pier and the broad green which faces it. Bear right towards Brixham before Paignton harbour and pass Goodrington Station. This is on the Paignton and Dartmouth Railway.

Continue to head towards Brixham. At Galmpton the Torbay ring-road leaves to the right, but keep on through Churston Ferrers on to the spacious common. After the golf club there is a junction with the A379 which goes to the Dartmouth ferries. Remain on the Brixham road to reach traffic lights where you turn right A down Monksbridge Road following the sign to Berry Head. Turn left at the following roundabout and

• PLACES OF INTEREST •

Torquay

Torquay's history really began in the opening years of the nineteenth century. The English fleet, continually ready for war, often sheltered in Tor Bay in preference to Plymouth Sound. Because of this, many naval officers established their families in nearby villas. The climate was found to be beneficial for diseases such as consumption. At the same time sea bathing became fashionable.

Because of the war with France it was not possible for people to travel to the continent for holidays, and many began to rent accommodation here. When the war ended Torquay continued to expand, with more fine houses being built for well-to-do patrons. Nevertheless, it remained a remote place. The railway arrived in 1848 and, until then, it had been difficult to reach Torquay from London. The resort expanded, but continued to be a place for the wealthy. It became known as 'the Montpellier of England'. More and more large houses were built amongst the trees on the slopes above the waterfront. Following the contours in an informal way they gave Torquay its continental character which it retained until after the Second World War.

Not surprisingly, after a hundred years or so, many of the original houses started to age. From the 1960s onwards they began to be replaced with tall apartment blocks which, though not destroying the town's appearance, certainly altered it greatly. Of course, Torquay is no longer a resort reserved solely for the wealthy, although it does have its share of de luxe accommodation. It has developed to meet the demands of an ever-changing holiday market.

Luxury yachts jostle for berths in the harbour, just as motorists vie for spaces in the car parks. The hotels and grand houses of yesteryear have become holiday flats, nursing homes or have vanished altogether. Yet nothing can destroy the town's enduring beauty – red cliffs contrasting with the azure blue of the bay.

Paignton and Dartmouth Steam Railway

Trains run along the former Great Western Railway between Paignton and Kingswear, a distance of 7 miles. The route allows views of Tor Bay and the Dart estuary. There is also the opportunity of combining a train ride with a river cruise. This is a good way of avoiding Dartmouth's parking problems! Services April–October and December. Telephone: (01803) 555872.

continue until you reach another set of traffic lights. Go straight over here towards Berry Head. Fork right to pass the rugby ground and a holiday village to reach Berry Head Country Park. There is a choice of walks here, either westwards into the town or southwards along the cliffs to Sharkham Point and beyond.

From the Berry Head Country Park retrace your steps to traffic lights in Higher Brixham. Turn left and climb the hill past the church. At the top turn right on to the A379 towards Paignton. There is a beautiful view of Tor Bay as the road dips down. **Take the unsignposted turning to the left B which comes just after a concealed car park on the left. At the junction itself there is a yellow grit container by the roadside.** This road does not appear promising at first, it looks almost like a layby or a farm track, but it soon improves.

A train at Kingswear on the Paignton and Dartmouth Railway

Cross the railway to reach a T-junction where you turn right into Galmpton. Turn left at The Roundings, just beyond the school and village hall, and then left again to pass the post office on the left, heading for Stoke Gabriel. Climb a steep hill to come to the tiny village of Waddeton. Pink cottages are grouped around the crossroads at its centre.

Follow the signs here for Stoke Gabriel and, at the next crossroads turn left into the village. Keep on the main road and take a turning to the right which leads down to a delightful car park by the river. There is a good view of the church from here. The church has a medieval painted screen which, like the church itself, has been much restored. The yew tree standing close to the church is supposed to be a thousand years old.

Return through the village and pass the Village

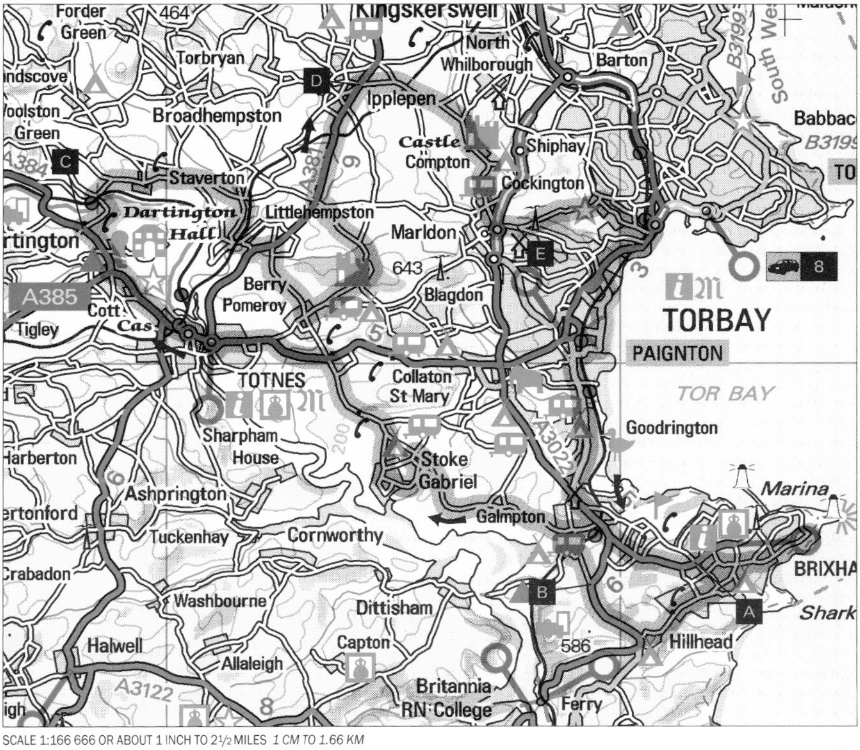

SCALE 1:166 666 OR ABOUT 1 INCH TO 2½ MILES *1 CM TO 1.66 KM*

Cockington village makes a popular excursion from Torquay

Shop. Follow the main road round to the right towards Paignton and Totnes and then, after 200 yards (183 m), turn left to Aish. Turn left at a T-junction and then carry straight on at the next junction. The road broadens a little after this. **Pass through Aish to come to the A385 where you turn left into Totnes.**

Take the first exit at the roundabout and then, having crossed the River Dart, go right at the second roundabout taking the A385

• PLACES OF INTEREST •

Berry Head
Berry Head is the southern extremity of Tor Bay. The cliffs are an important breeding ground for colonies of sea-birds, notably guillemots, kittiwakes, fulmars and razorbills. The limestone cliffs are also important for their flora. The lighthouse is sometimes described as being the shortest and the highest in Britain. It is only twelve feet (3.6 m) high, but stands on top of a 200- (61 m) foot cliff. Berry Head was hazardous for sailors – 170 soldiers drowned in 1745 when their transport, the *Tiger*, broke up on its rocks. Also, in a gale on 10 January 1866 thirty vessels were wrecked in Tor Bay.

Paignton
Paignton is ancient – its market charter dates from 1295. The town was formerly known for its cabbages and cider. The railway reached the sleepy fishing village in 1859, and from then on it continued to expand until the early years of the twentieth century.

Paignton is now a seaside town with a sandy beach and all the facilities which might be expected to go with it. Yet, away from the shore there is much of interest. Sixteenth-century cottages can be found at the centre of the old village around the church. The church contains wonderful monuments in the fifteenth-century Kirkham Chantry.

The council occupies Oldway House, a mansion put up by Isaac Singer (founder of the sewing-machine empire) and enlarged by his son in 1907 to rival Versailles. In complete contrast, Kirkham House is a late-medieval house, originally built by a well-off farmer or merchant. It has been immaculately restored and furnished.

Berry Pomeroy Castle
The castle is one of the most romantic ruins in England, its shattered ramparts stand at the top of a tree-shrouded cliff. The land once belonged to a great Norman family, the de Pomeroys who

extended this stronghold in the late fourteenth century. In 1547 the castle was bought by Edward Seymour, Duke of Somerset, who was later Lord Protector in the reign of Edward VI before being beheaded in 1552. He began considerable improvements, which were continued by his son, to make the castle commodious as well as impregnable.

The house was occupied until after 1688, but was abandoned soon after and left to become a picturesque ruin. The most complete part still standing is the gatehouse with a chapel in the upper chamber. There are also sections of the south and west ramparts. Be careful when exploring these, however, as the ghost of the evil Lady Margaret Pomeroy, who murdered her sister, is supposed to push people off the wall into the ravine below! (English Heritage).

Open daily April–September 10–6. October 10–4. Telephone: (01803) 863397.

Compton Castle
The castle is still occupied by the Gilbert family who, in the fourteenth century, built a small manor house here. This is now at the heart of the house which was enlarged and fortified by John Gilbert c. 1520. The fortifications, though impressive, were for show rather than to serve any practical purpose, but they give the castle its romantic appeal. The great hall of the medieval house was carefully reconstructed in 1955. (National Trust). Courtyard, restored great hall, solar, chapel, rose garden and old kitchen can be seen.

Open April–October Mondays, Wednesdays and Thursdays 10–12.15 and 2–5. Telephone: (01803)872112.

out of Totnes. The castle is to the left as the road climbs past the station, the terminus of the South Devon Railway. **Where the road divides take the right turn to stay on the A385 to reach Dartington. At the roundabout take the A384 towards Buckfastleigh.** The Dartington Cider Press Craft Centre is to the right and the church and the entrance to Dartington Hall is a little further on.

About 1/2 mile past Dartington church take the turning to the right C to Staverton Bridge and Broadhempston. The beautiful seven-arched bridge dates from 1413. This is followed immediately by a level-crossing. **Turn right after this and then right again when a road to Landscove goes to the left.** Pass the Sea Trout Inn in the attractive village of Staverton. The church is down a cul-de-sac to the right. **Climb out of the village on the main road and fork right at Blacklersland Cross towards Littlehempston. Keep straight on at Copper Tree Cross and then fork right at Reeveacre Cross to Littlehempston and Buckyette. Keep straight on when the major road swings away to the left and crosses a bridge.** You are now on the right side of the valley with the railway close to the left.

Stoke Gabriel stands on a creek off the River Dart

At Littlehempston turn left to cross a little bridge over the river and then go under the railway bridge. Bear right towards Totnes. At the A381 turn left towards Newton Abbot to pass the Pig and Whistle Inn and then take the first turn right to Berry Pomeroy (this is quite an acute turn). The road with its overhanging trees soon reaches Berry Pomeroy. **Turn left at the mini-roundabout. Bear left at the next junction following the sign towards Berry Pomeroy Castle and Afton.** The drive to the castle is on the left.

Carry on along this lane. It is narrow and enclosed, but carries little traffic. It is worth pausing at a gateway on the left to enjoy a view of the countryside, although you will not see the castle from here. **Carry straight on when a road leaves to the right.** After this the lane descends into woodland. **Bear left when the road divides after a causeway. Climb the hill keeping on the major road. Turn right to Newton Abbot on to the A381. At the second set of crossroads, just before a pub, turn right D to Wrigwell and Dainton. Ignore the immediate turn to the right which goes to Wrigwell and head for Dainton. At the T-junction at Dainton Elm turn right towards Compton and Marldon. Follow the National Trust signs down a steep embanked lane into Compton.**

Compton Castle is to the right and can be seen from the road. The long straggling village almost joins with Marldon. **Keep straight ahead to reach a roundabout. Turn left here to reach another roundabout on the A380. Go straight over here towards Preston. After about 1/4 mile turn left E to Cockington, on a lane unsuitable for coaches.** The road descends steeply. There is a good view over Tor Bay. The car park for Cockington is on the left as you come into the village. **Bear right around the square and then take the second exit to climb a steeply-banked lane. At the end of the lane bear right to return to the seafront.** ■

Compton Castle, one of Devon's loveliest houses

• TOUR 9 •

ASHBURTON, BUCKLAND IN THE MOOR AND TWO BRIDGES

35 MILES – 2 HOURS
START AND FINISH AT ASHBURTON

This tour, though short, provides an excellent flavour of Dartmoor. It uses quiet lanes through countryside which is off the beaten track. However, the drive still takes you to many well-known beauty spots – the villages of Widecombe and Buckland, the riverside at Postbridge and Huccaby Bridge and, as a grand finale, Buckfast Abbey.

Pass Ashburton's town hall and car park to the left and turn left over the bridge to Widecombe and Buckland in the Moor. The lane climbs steadily out of the town. There is woodland at the top of the hill where the road levels. **A road leads off to the right to Haytor and Widecombe. Keep straight on A to Buckland.** The ground rises steeply to the right of the road to Buckland Beacon, best reached by going straight on at A. At 1,250 feet (381 m) this is a magnificent viewpoint. The Ten Commandments Stone at the top, composed of two granite slabs, was inscribed with text in 1928 under the prompting of the local squire. The same man had the words 'My dear Mother' put on Buckland's church clock instead of numerals.

As the lane approaches the village it passes through beautiful

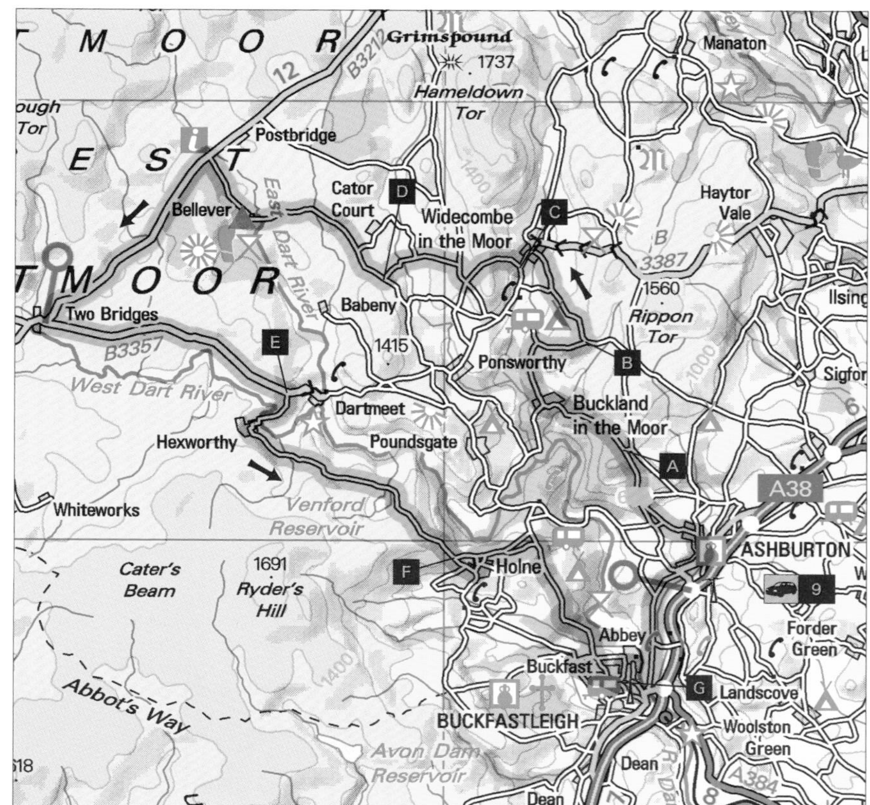

SCALE 1:166 666 OR ABOUT 1 INCH TO 2½ MILES *1 CM TO 1.66 KM*

Buckfast Abbey is a grand monument to the faith and perseverance of its Benedictine monks

beech woods. A craft centre occupies the Round House with workshops, a gift shop and a café. After this the road drops very steeply to the celebrated part of the village with its thatched cottages grouped around a stream. The road then climbs to pass the church on the left. **Continue to a T-junction at Stone Cross and turn right.** The lane soon reaches open moorland. **Turn sharply left B at the next junction at Pudsham Down.**

The road descends to the hamlet of Venton. There are lots of places along the broad, grassy verges where you can stop to enjoy the moorland views. Pony-trekkers use this lane as access to the moors. As the road begins to descend you can see Widecombe church – there can be few more beautifully-situated churches in England.

Bear right at Chittleford Cross to pass the Rugglestone Inn. The road comes out in the middle of Widecombe. Turn left to pass the post office. After about 1/4 mile up the hill turn right C to Southcombe. This road continues the steep climb to the moor. Footpaths go along the crest of the moor and provide fine views of Widecombe and beyond. There is usually an abundance of yellow gorse which photographers can use as a foreground to a classic moorland scene. A little further on the view from the road opens up westwards and provides another superb panorama of Dartmoor.

Turn right at the crossroads and then take the first left to Broadaford and Cator. This is a delightful little lane with broad verges and fields on either

• *PLACES OF INTEREST* •

Ashburton

Ashburton gets its name from the River Ashburn which hurries through the town to join with the Dart at Buckfast. It is an ancient town and belonged to the bishops of Exeter until the reign of James I. Its charter dates from 1238, but it had a market well before this. Later it became one of Dartmoor's four stannary towns. Tin mining and woollen production brought in the revenue to enable the church to be rebuilt early in the fifteenth century. Its tower is 92 feet (28 m) high, and it so impressed the citizens of Totnes that they copied it for their own church which was built in 1449.

After the middle of the seventeenth century road transport became of greater importance. Ashburton's position, midway between Exeter and Plymouth, led to its development as a coaching centre. Horses were changed and passengers dined and rested here. However, Celia Fiennes, an experienced traveller, found it a poor little town in 1698 – she wrote that 'bad was the best Inn'.

Many of the town's most attractive buildings date from this time. However, it is sometimes difficult to appreciate their age as, in the traditional Devon manner, their fronts have been hung with slates.

Ashburton declined when the railway made travelling easier and faster. The branch railway linking it to Totnes opened in 1872, but failed to boost the town's fortunes. Its other industries, as well as the market, also wilted, and for a century or so it became a quiet backwater. It was revived when the rise of the private car boosted tourism and brought visitors eager to explore Dartmoor. Today, it is the largest town within the boundaries of the Dartmoor National Park.

Hexworthy Bridge over the West Dart River

side. **Keep on the main road when minor lanes go off to different farms. Go over the tiny bridge which crosses the West Webburn River. Be ready to turn sharply left through stone gate-posts to keep on the major road when a byway goes straight ahead.** Beech trees flank this road, their roots standing up above the banks as though preparing to walk.

The lane winds through a farmyard at Cator and then climbs steeply to reach Cator Green. **Turn right here D to Bellever.** The road crosses a bridge by a moorland stream where there is room to park for a picnic. The road dips into the forest and crosses the East Dart River. Just after this there is a Forestry Commission parking place to the left. Waymarked

• PLACES OF INTEREST •

Widecombe in the Moor
It is easy to see why Widecombe church, with its tall tower topped by proportionately-high pinnacles, is called 'the cathedral of the moor'. Whichever way you approach the village the church dominates. It stands at the centre of one of the largest of all parishes, covering 11,000 acres. In contrast to the tower, in typical West Country manner, the rest of the church is long and low, and was built in the fourteenth century, nearly two hundred years before the tower. The inside of the building has a simple grandeur. It has beautifully-proportioned arches, and the remains of the rood-screen still bear medieval paintings. In the tower there are four boards painted in 1786 with verses describing the thunderstorm on 21 October 1638. Lightning struck the church during afternoon service and killed four people and injured sixty-two others. The incident also highlights the size of the congregations in those days.

On the western side of the church there is a little square with the Church House to the left. The house was built in 1537 as a brewhouse and subsequently became the village school. It now belongs to the National Trust and is used as the village hall. The adjacent Sexton's Cottage serves as a Dartmoor National Park Information Centre and National Trust shop.

Widecombe Fair, immortalised in song, takes place on the second Tuesday in September.

Hembury Castle
Not to be confused with the much grander Hembury Fort close to Honiton. This is an Iron Age hill-fort commanding the approach up the Dart valley. At its western end the Normans built a small motte-and-bailey castle, using the ramparts of the hill-fort as an outer bailey.

Buckfast Abbey
The first monastery on this site was founded in 1018. After the Conquest this grew to become the wealthiest Cistercian abbey in south-west England. After the Dissolution the abbey was quickly made ruinous by a landowner who stripped it of all usable building materials. In 1806 Samuel Berry, a local mill owner, put up a Gothic mansion on the site.

The most important year in the history of the abbey was 1882 when French and German Benedictine monks moved to Buckfast from France. They established a community which became autonomous in 1902 when the first abbot was chosen. The monks occupied Berry's mansion at first, but soon began to build themselves a magnificent church. They started it in 1907, following the medieval ground plan, and the building was consecrated twenty five years later, a triumph for the four monks principally involved in the building. The abbey still serves as a Benedictine monastery, although many commercial activities have been established to keep it in funds. It has its own restaurant and shop where products of the abbey (such as honey and tonic wine) can be bought together with countless other items. It is also the venue for concerts and conferences.

Open daily 5.30 am–9.30 pm. Telephone: (01364) 42519

walks lead into the forest.

The road turns sharply to the right and passes a row of white houses as it climbs the hill at Bellever. When you reach the main road at Postbridge turn left towards Two Bridges on the B3212. The car park, information centre and famous clapper bridge are all to the right at this junction. The chimney of the abandoned Powder Mills can be seen to the right a little further along the B3212 as you crest the rise, after the forest ends to the left. The neighbouring cottages now house a pottery and craft centre. This is the infamous stretch of road known for a manifestation called the Hairy Hands, supposed to wrench the steering wheel away from you with calamitous results!

The television mast on Hessary Tor is seen ahead as the road approaches Two Bridges. **When you meet the B3357 turn left.** Bellever Tor can be seen perched above woodland to the left. There are plenty of parking places. As the road crosses the Cherry Brook there are views to the right down to the West Dart River. **Before you reach Dartmeet take the only turn to the right E, signposted to Hexworthy and Venford Reservoir, to drop down to Hexworthy Bridge.** Parking is extremely limited at this beauty spot. On the other side of the bridge the road climbs to the Forest Inn.

Continue along the main road signposted to Holne. About 1/2 mile further on there is a wonderful panorama from Combestone Tor northwards over the River Dart. As the road begins to dip to Venford Reservoir you can see the sea in the distance. The reservoir was built in 1907 to supply Paignton and Teignmouth. There are parking places by the reservoir, both before and after the dam.

Follow the road into Holne village, forking right F at the junction after the reservoir. Holne has a pub, a tearoom at the Old Forge, and a car park near its beautiful church. Charles Kingsley was born here in 1819 when his father was the curate of the village.

The view from Comberstone Tor

Head straight over the crossroads at the Church House Inn following the sign to Ashburton and Princetown. Join the road which runs above the village by turning right and then, when the road divides, taking the right-hand fork to Hembury. The road winds through pleasant woodlands before meeting with a road from the left from Ashburton. **Bear right here, still heading for Hembury.** This junction has the romantic name of 'Gallant Le Bower'. There are walks through the woods to Holne Bridge. As the road descends wonderful views open up. Hembury Woods are to the left. There is a National Trust parking place from which you can walk to Hembury Castle.

When you come to a T-junction turn right to reach Hockmoorhead crossroads. Turn left here and then fork left again to follow the main road down into Buckfast. Turn left G at Round Cross when the road to the parish church is straight ahead. The tower of the abbey is seen as the road drops to a small roundabout. The entrance to the abbey is to the left just before this.

Turn right at the roundabout to pass the mill shop. Continue past the carpet factory and the Abbey Inn, and then turn left on to the main road. After the bridge turn left again to Ashburton and Princetown. This stretch of road was part of the old A38 and will take you to the centre of Ashburton. ■

• TOUR 10 •

TEIGNMOUTH, LITTLE HALDON AND POWDERHAM CASTLE

38 MILES – 2 HOURS
START AND FINISH AT TEIGNMOUTH

This route takes you through Torquay, with its varied attractions, to the sandy heights of Little Haldon, overlooking Teignmouth from the north. Forest glades form a pleasing contrast as the tour continues to Great Haldon. The return follows the shore of the Exe estuary, passing Powderham Castle and Dawlish Warren.

From Teignmouth cross over Shaldon Bridge on the B3199 to Torquay. This was originally a toll bridge. It was built in 1825, from timber, and was the longest in the world, measuring 1,671 feet (509 m). It was rebuilt in steel and concrete in 1930 with twenty-three fixed spans and a central drawbridge. From the bridge there are fine views of the wide river and the Dartmoor hills beyond. There is also a wonderful view of Teignmouth as you climb out of Shaldon. There is a car park to the left from where you can walk to the tip of Shaldon Ness.

The coast road runs on the top of the cliffs. After a mile there is a viewpoint car park. From here you can see towards Babbacombe in one direction and across Lyme Bay in the other.

There is parking to the left in the village of Maidencombe. **Keep to the coast road through St Marychurch, following the signs to 'The Harbour' over two roundabouts.** A cliff railway takes passengers down to Oddicombe beach. **Continue through Babbacombe, passing turnings on the left to Anstey's Cove and Kent's Cavern.** As you get nearer to the centre of the town, along Babbacombe Road, there are several charming, mid-Victorian buildings. The road passes Torquay Museum (purpose-built between 1874 and 1876) and then continues its descent to the harbour. **Pass the clock tower and keep along the seafront past the Princess Theatre. Turn right A by the Grand Hotel to pass the station on the left. The one-way street joins Avenue Road, part of the A3022 which links Torquay and Newton Abbot.** This is a straightforward way out of town, although often very busy.

Follow the signs to Newton Abbot, eventually reaching a large roundabout where the

• PLACES OF INTEREST •

Teignmouth
The town is best viewed from Shaldon Ness at high tide. The eye naturally focuses on the graceful tower of St Michael's Church, situated almost on the beach with tree-clad, red cliffs rising up behind. From the Ness the town appears to be almost surrounded by water. The river is directly below, and the town covers a sandy spit reaching into the sea.

Teignmouth was one of the first South Devon towns to develop as a resort and, in 1803, was described as a 'fashionable watering place'. The railway reached the town in 1846. By this time its seafront had rows of respectable Regency houses which contrasted with the quays and warehouses of the busy riverfront immediately behind. Later, the esplanade and pier were built with quite a few imposing Victorian hotels. Teignmouth suffered badly from bombing raids during the Second World War, 79 people were killed and 151 wounded – a high percentage of its wartime population. This was not the first time it had suffered because of war. Twice the town had been left in flames by the French, in 1340 and 1690.

Kent's Cavern, Wellswood, Torquay. (Off the B3199, 1½ miles from town centre). This famous show cave is one of the most important archaeological sites in England. It has afforded shelter to man and beast over the past 350,000 years.

Open daily April–June and September–October 10–6. July and August 10–9 (6 on Saturdays). November–March 10–5. Last tour forty-five minutes before closing.

Telephone: (01803) 294059 or 215136

A3022 meets the A380. Bear right to head towards Exeter, crossing the River Teign on the outskirts of Newton Abbot. Leave the dual carriageway to take the A381 towards Teignmouth. After ¼ mile take the first turning on the left B, Combesend Road East, where a sign points to a Waste Disposal Site. This road soon passes the landfill site and descends into a wooded valley. **Keep to the main road at Colway Cross and continue ahead at the crossroads which follows.** This road climbs into woodland.

Turn left at the road junction at Little Haldon towards the Elizabethan Inn. There is a golf course to the right at the top of Little Haldon. **Keep straight on at the next crossroads.** Several car parks give access to the paths across the heath. **Cross straight over the B3192 following the signs to Ashcombe and Dawlish.** There are few places to park after this.

Carry on over the next crossroads to enter woodland, still heading for Ashcombe. As the woods thin out there are views over the Exe estuary. **Do not be distracted by these views as you need to take a small lane on the left C marked only by a sign limiting the weight of vehicles to 17 tonnes.** This narrow twisting lane dips down steeply. There are fine views over fields of red earth dotted with woodland. An obelisk stands in the woods on the other side of the valley in the Mamhead estate. It was erected in 1742 as a daymark for shipping. **Turn right and then left to cross a main road at Ashcombe, heading towards Mamhead. Keep straight over another crossroads by Westley Manor.**

The lane climbs up into more dense woodland. There is a busy picnic place at the top, the starting point for the Mamhead

Teignmouth's picturesque riverfront

Forest walks. **At a crossroads turn right D towards Mamhead and Starcross.** There is another car park to the left just after this junction. Pass the entrance to Mamhead House, one of Devon's major country houses. It was built between 1826 and 1835 by Anthony Salvin in parkland landscaped earlier by Capability Brown. **After two crossroads turn left at the next junction E to Kenton.**

The lane reaches the village, facing a magnificent red sandstone church, so close to the road that you could almost drive into it. As in most south Devon

• PLACES OF INTEREST •

Torre Abbey, King's Drive, Torquay
The abbey stands in.beautiful gardens close to the seafront. At the time of the Dissolution it was the wealthiest Premonstratensian house in the country. Only the great tithe barn and gatehouse remain of the monastery. The abbey became the family home of the Carys who adapted it as their mansion in Georgian times. Twenty of its rooms are open to the public, including the dining-room and family chapel. There are mementoes of Agatha Christie who belonged to the Cary family.

Open Easter–October daily 9.30–6. Telephone: (01803) 293593.

Powderham Castle
The castle has been the home of the Courtenay family, Earls of Devon, for six hundred years. At the heart of the building lies a medieval manor house but, through the centuries, this has grown into the baronial stronghold we see today. When it was built the river extended much further inland and practically lapped

against the castle walls. Its defensive strength was tested during the Civil War when the royalist garrison held out for six weeks against the besieging parliamentarians before being forced to surrender.

In the eighteenth century substantial alterations were carried out for the second Viscount. A beautiful Music Room was added but, between 1845 and 1847, the castle was thoroughly transformed by the tenth Earl. He engaged Charles Fowler to enlarge and embellish Powderham so that it faced inland, rather than towards the railway, then under construction. Powderham contains many fine pieces of furniture and a fascinating collection of portraits reflect the long history of the Courtenay family here.

Open April–September daily except Saturdays 10–5.30.

Starcross
Starcross is a small village facing Exmouth on the other side of the estuary. There is a pedestrian ferry in the summer linking it to the resort.

One of its pubs is named the Atmospheric Railway, after Brunel's bold scheme which he intended to use on his railway to Plymouth in 1844. He thought that the locomotives of the day would not be powerful enough to take the trains up the steep gradients, and so invented a system in which a piston was mounted underneath a carriage of a train. The piston ran inside a tube from which air was exhausted by the pumping station, leather seals closing as the train passed. The scheme proved to be a disastrous failure because water and rats destroyed the vital leather seals on which the system depended. It cost the South Devon Railway Company £400,000, a vast sum at the time for shareholders to cover. One of the pump houses, built at intervals of 3 miles along the line, stands on the seaward side of the road. Until recently it served as a museum illustrating the operation of the atmospheric railway.

Dawlish
You have to look inland from the seafront to sample the true flavour of Dawlish, the town which attracted Jane Austen and Dickens (who made it the birthplace of Nicholas Nickleby). It takes its name from its river, known to the Saxons as Doflisc, 'the black stream'. Its earliest charter dates from 1044 and, for the next seven centuries, seems to have been a thriving little seaport. A fine medieval church was built 1/2 mile inland at the centre of the village. In 1301 Dawlish was called upon to supply a ship and men to fight in the Scottish wars, a call repeated in 1513.

Dawlish's appeal as a resort probably dates from the early 1790s. In 1790 the banker, Charles Hoare, bought land above the village. He engaged John Nash and Humphrey Repton (who were then in partnership) to build Luscombe Castle. He hoped that the place 'where summer lingers and spring pays her earliest visits' would improve the health of his ailing wife.

In the early years of the nineteenth century the stream was straightened to run through a wide lawn. The Strand and Brunswick Place were created to overlook it. It is strange that at Dawlish the fashionable houses of the time had nothing to do with the sea, and looked towards each other across the little valley. Elsewhere, at Teignmouth and Brighton, terraces and crescents were being built with sea views. In Victorian times, however, the popularity of Dawlish continued to grow, in spite of its separation from the seafront by the embankment of the railway. It remains a fine place for holidaymakers – sunbathers love its secluded coves, and children enjoy the sands and the covered, heated swimming pool.

The stream runs through The Lawn at Dawlish

churches, the tower was the last part to be built (early sixteenth century) and is 120 feet (37 m) high. **Turn right and then, at the village green, right again on to the A379 towards Starcross and Dawlish. You pass the entrance to Powderham Castle on the left before leaving Kenton.**

After Starcross a road leaves to the right to Mamhead. Take the turn to the left F a few yards after this, signposted to Eastdon, and cross a small causeway. There is a little harbour here, picturesque when the tide is in.

The road heads through Eastdon to Dawlish Warren, a sand spit which juts out into the Exe estuary. This is a nature reserve where rare waders, such as avocets (their peculiar cry makes them known as 'yelpers') can occasionally be seen. More common species are dunlin, widgeon and brent-geese. It is also the only British habitat of the sand crocus. The Warren's sandy beach is popular in summer, but you will find the crowds thin out as you approach the end of the spit. If you wish to visit the Warren there are car parks to the left of the road on each side of the station.

The road leads past caravan and camping sites to rejoin the A379 which soon reaches Dawlish. From here the return to Teignmouth is by the coast road (B3199). Unfortunately, many views from here are concealed by housing. ■

Torquay harbour at dusk

• TOUR 11 •

DARTMOUTH, START POINT AND SLAPTON SANDS

40 MILES – 2 HOURS
START AND FINISH AT DARTMOUTH

The South Hams is the area of South Devon between the rivers Dart and Plym. It is bounded by Dartmoor to the north and the coast to the south. This drive discovers some of its hidden villages, passing through rich farmland, characteristic of the district. It is an area of leafy hedges, pockets of dense woodland, and small fields. The route negotiates some rather tortuous lanes by the creeks of the Kingsbridge estuary and then follows the coast passing Start Point and Slapton Sands. If you reach South Pool at high tide a diversion can be made to East Prawle.

The tour starts from Dartmouth's Higher Ferry. Take the A379 (Kingsbridge and Totnes road) to climb the hill past the Naval College. Keep on the main road towards Totnes when the A379 goes off to the left. Just beyond this junction the car park for the Dartmouth park-and-ride is to the left. After about 4 miles you will pass the Sportsman's Arms at Hemborough Post where the main road bends to the left. **Drive on for 3/4 mile and then, before the Dartmouth Golf and Country Club, take the sharp turn to the left A signposted to Blackawton and Slapton. Fork right immediately to Blackawton.** This was one of the villages evacuated at the time of the rehearsals for the D-Day landings.

The road descends into a very attractive, wooded valley. Soon afterwards it reaches Blackawton with its two pubs, one appropriately named the Normandy Arms. It also has a very large and attractive church. The chancel dates from 1333, but the rest is mainly late fifteenth century. There is a beautiful Norman font with honeysuckle ornamentation and a screen which bears the emblems and colours of Henry VIII and Catherine of Aragon.

After the church go straight on towards Millcombe, passing the post office. This narrow lane, with grass down the middle, descends into a little valley, typical of this district. At the bottom you reach a crossroads by a farm house. **Go straight over to Abbotsleigh and Slapton. When you reach a T-junction at Bow Cross turn right, following the main road signposted to East Allington and Kingsbridge. Keep on the main road at Newton Cross by bearing right. At Wallaton Cross go straight over towards a trout farm, heading for Sherford and Kingsbridge.**

At Cole's Cross B ignore the first turning to the left and turn left at the T-junction which follows immediately. Then bear left again at Kingsbridgefork Cross, heading for a cider press as well as a trout farm. A lane to the trout farm and Stokenham goes off to the left, but you keep on towards Sherford and Frogmore.

At the next crossroads (Stancombe Cross) continue ahead, unless you wish to visit the cider press, in which case turn left. The route descends into Sherford. The church appears to be built of

The Sherman tank at Torcross is a reminder of a wartime tragedy

• PLACES OF INTEREST •

Dartmouth
The town's appeal is primarily its situation. There is little level ground here and the houses rise up from the waterfront in tiers, enjoying superlative views of the river.

Dartmouth has many fine buildings reflecting its long, and often violent, history. It grew to be one of England's busiest seaports in the twelfth century, when trade with France was boosted by Henry II's marriage – wine from Bordeaux being the major import.

The fleets which carried knights to the first and second Crusades assembled at Dartmouth, but peace with France never lasted long. In 1346 Dartmouth supplied Edward III with thirty-one ships for the siege of Calais – only Fowey and Yarmouth sent more.

'A fortalice by the sea' was built to protect the town against raiders. Only fragments of this remain, situated above the Lower Ferry.

Dartmouth Castle was built between 1481 and 1495 to face Kingswear Castle on the other side of the river. A great chain was forged to stretch across the river and could be raised if enemy ships threatened to approach. The castle was amongst the first to be designed for artillery. The delightful church of St Petrox stands within its grounds. The town's other church, St Saviour's, was built on the site of a harbour-side chapel consecrated in 1286.

A great boost to the town came at the end of the sixteenth century when Dartmouth's fishermen began their annual voyages to the Newfoundland fishing grounds. At the same time exports of woollens revived. Dartmouth merchants and ship-owners became prosperous and they built fine houses, still to be seen around The Quay. Four of their extravagantly-decorated, timber-framed houses compose the Butterwalk.

Dartmouth declined as a port in the eighteenth and nineteenth centuries. During the first part of the twentieth century it depended on the Royal Naval College (built between 1899 and 1905) as well as boat-building. Today, the rise of private pleasure-boating and water sport has provided the town with a new clientele, though it will always attract those with an interest in history, architecture and fine scenery.

Dartmouth Castle (English Heritage). Open April–September daily 10–6. October–March Wednesday–Sunday 10–4. Telephone: (01803) 833588

Dartmouth Museum, 6 Butterwalk. Beautiful seventeenth-century merchant's house contains maritime museum.

Open November–Easter Monday– Saturday 1.15–4. Easter–October Monday–Saturday 11–5. Telephone: (01803) 832923

Newcomen Memorial Engine, Mayors Avenue. Thomas Newcomen (1663–1729) was a citizen of Dartmouth and many credit him with the invention of the steam engine.

Open April– September Monday–Saturday 9.30–5.30, Sunday 10–4. October–March Monday–Saturday 9.30–4.30. Telephone: (01803) 834224 or 834959

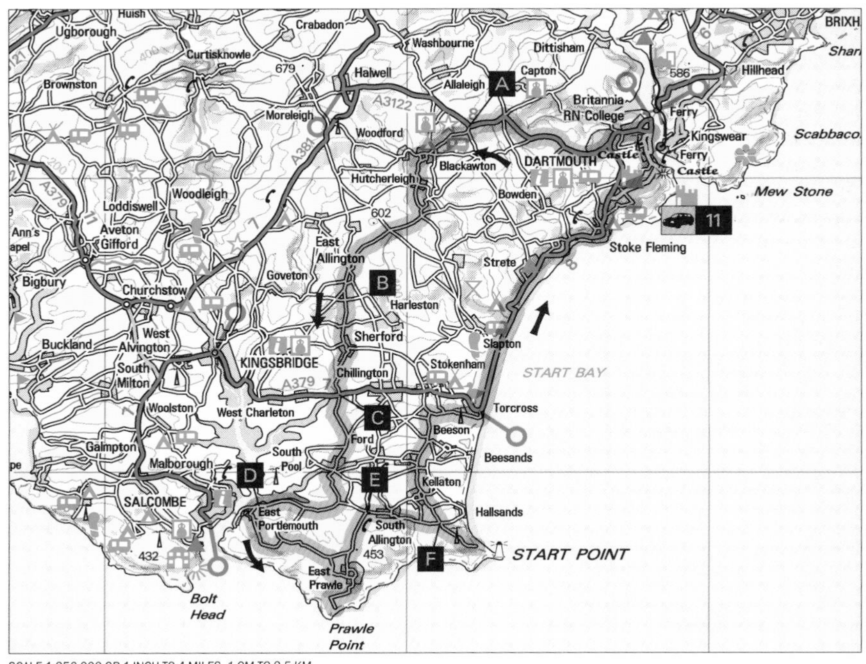

SCALE 1:250 000 OR 1 INCH TO 4 MILES *1 CM TO 2.5 KM*

• PLACES OF INTEREST •

The South Hams
This area is a peninsula bounded by the rivers Dart and Plym and backed by Dartmoor. It has always been an agricultural district – cattle and sheep were taken up to the moor in the summer and brought home in winter to lowland pastures. They used to raise large breeds of cattle, South Devons or the local South Hammers, fit to work as oxen. They would drag the plough through thick red clay which matched the colour of their pelts.

Time seems to run at a less hectic rate in the South Hams (especially in the part away from the coast) than elsewhere, and old values still hold good.

In 1943 the rural idyll was brutally disrupted when tens of thousands of allied troops descended on the district so that they could prepare for the D-day landings. Villages were evacuated and left deserted until after the invasion, and those locals remaining were only allowed to do so under a cloak of utmost secrecy.

Hallsands
For centuries Hallsands, with its cottages perched on a rock platform, was a thriving community. It was famous for its crab fishing but, in 1897, an entrepreneur began dredging gravel from the seabed, just offshore, to supply material for extending the dockyard at Devonport. This did away with the natural sea defences and the ledge on which Hallsands was built was undermined. Terrible storms in January 1917 destroyed twenty-nine of its thirty houses, miraculously without loss of life. One little old lady was left in the only remaining cottage. She refused to leave her home and occupied it until her death in 1964.

It is possible to scramble over the rocks to examine the remains of the houses, but you have to be fairly athletic to do so!

Slapton Sands
A two-mile-long shingle beach separates the sea from Slapton Ley, the largest freshwater lake in Devon. Two nature trails have been marked out for visitors.

At the Torcross end of the lake, a Sherman tank stands menacingly on a plinth. It is an unofficial reminder of a disaster which occurred during the rehearsals for the D-day landings. A convoy of landing-craft was allowed to sail unescorted into Lyme Bay and was caught by German E-boats. A total of 946 American soldiers died, and the fiasco was so successfully covered up that it remained secret until the 1970s. At the mid-point of the beach there is an official stone monument.

Start Point
The headland at the southern end of Tor Bay always held a threat to sailing ships. Sheltered waters lie to the north and the coast westwards is rocky and hazardous. The lighthouse, built in 1836, failed to prevent the four collisions which occurred off the headland in 1854, two hundred lives being lost in one of them.

It is easy to imagine such tragedies if you walk on these cliffs on a stormy day, but on a quiet summer's day all seems serene.

greyish, lichen-covered stone but, in fact, it is constructed entirely of slate. Sherford is a long village straggling along the lane towards the A379 at Frogmore.

Turn right at the main road and then, after 100 yards (91 m), left C to head for South Pool and East Prawle. There is a glimpse of Frogmore Creek after you turn off the main road. **Keep ahead on the main road when roads go off to the left to East Prawle and East Portlemouth.** The road descends very steeply into South Pool. **Ignore the road to the left to East Prawle** (unless the tide is high when you may have to divert here to go via East Prawle to reach East Portlemouth) **and keep ahead to Waterhead and East Portlemouth, passing the notice which warns that the road can be flooded at high tide.** The switchback road eventually reaches a creek (known as Goodshelter) where it crosses a ford. It then follows the side of the creek, giving a succession of views, to East Portlemouth.

If you wish to see the waterfront fork right D towards Mill Bay. At busy times it will be difficult to find parking places in this cul-de-sac. A passenger ferry to Salcombe leaves from the shore before you get to Mill Bay.

Turn sharply to the left when the road divides and climb to Godolphin Corner where you will find the village

Blackpool Sands near Dartmouth

Dartmouth's inner harbour

stores. A footpath descends to the ferry from here. **Pass the shop and then bear right at the church to Rickham.** This lane threads through steep banks. Go past Rickham Farm and a sign to Gara Rock Hotel. **Turn right at the T-junction at Rickham Cross to East Prawle and Stokenham. The junction at Viniver's Cross may come as a bit of a surprise. Turn right here to East Prawle.** At the next T-junction, just before the village at Higher Farm, you may like to turn right to a car park on Prawle Point. From here the Coastal Path provides access to a wonderful stretch of cliff scenery.

Otherwise, continue by turning left towards Kingsbridge. Keep on the main road after the village. At this point the road can actually accommodate two cars side-by-side! However, it soon narrows again. **At a staggered cross-roads E turn right to South Allington. At a T-junction turn right on to a very narrow lane.** This follows the valley into woodland at the bottom. **Turn right at the T-junction (Lannacombe Green) to take the lane signposted to Start Point and South Hallsands.** If you wish to visit Lannacombe Beach take the turn to the right which follows immediately. There is a car park at the end of the lane.

The route continues by turning left to reach the crossroads at Hollowcombehead Cross F. If you wish to visit Start Point, turn right to the car park at the end of the lane near the lighthouse. From here there is a choice of walks, either to the tip of the headland or along the coastal path in either direction.

Otherwise, turn left at the crossroads. The next turn to the right leads to Bickerton only. The second goes to Hallsands – there is a car park at the end of the lane.

After the turn to Hallsands keep ahead to join a main road at Dunstone Cross, bearing right to head towards Stokenham to reach Mattiscombe Cross. Turn sharply right here. You get a fine vista over Slapton Sands as the lane descends steeply into Torcross. **When the lane joins the main road by the Village Inn, bear right.** This takes you northwards along the shingle bank with Slapton Ley to the left and the beach to the right. There is a car park on the left at the Torcross end of the lake (where a Sherman tank is displayed), one close to the monument further on and another at the end of the beach. **The road twists sharply to the left and climbs to the top of the cliff to reach the village of Strete.** After the village, the road approaches Blackpool Sands, a popular place for holidaymakers. In 1404 French soldiers from Brittany landed here in order to capture Dartmouth, but were beaten by citizens and sailors from the port. There is a large car park here, but note that dogs are forbidden in the car park and on the beach.

Drive on to Stoke Fleming. The church tower here has been a landmark for shipping for centuries. The road climbs out of the village past a garage. **Just after the camp site turn right following the brown sign to Dartmouth Castle.** The National Trust car park at Little Dartmouth is reached by turning right at the first crossroads. From here you can take a beautiful clifftop walk to the castle and the town.

Otherwise, keep ahead following the road down into Dartmouth. Pass the pottery to the right and a road which goes to the castle. Enjoy the excellent views of the waterfront as you descend into the town. ■

The lighthouse at Start Point is reached by a clifftop path

• TOUR 12 •

EXETER, GREAT HALDON AND THE TEIGN VALLEY

35 MILES – 2 HOURS
START AND FINISH AT EXETER

Binoculars are useful for this tour! It passes the estuary of the River Exe, noted for its abundance of wading birds, and visits the Birds of Prey Viewpoint in Haldon Forest. Later, the valley of the River Teign may provide sightings of dippers and kingfishers. Here you may also visit the Canonteign Falls, where there is a waterfall as well as lakes, ponds and wetland. All attract a wide range of wildlife.

Leave Exeter on the road to Dawlish (A379). The road passes beneath the motorway viaduct and the railway line is to the left with the canal just beyond. The village of Exminster is to the right just beyond the motorway. Pass a turning on the left which goes to Powderham village with its lovely church. (The castle is reached by continuing on the main road through Kenton.)

Descend through a cutting which is spanned by an iron footbridge. Just after this take the well-concealed turning to the right A signposted to Kennford and Kenn. This takes you over a flat stretch of countryside heading towards wooded hills. **Go straight over the crossroads at Willsworthy Cross to reach the village of Kenn. Just before the church turn left following the sign to Chudleigh and Newton Abbot. Cross the bridge over the River Kenn and then bear right to keep on the major road through the village.**

When you come to the A38 turn left, and then right, to cross the bridge over the dual carriageway. On the other side of the trunk road turn right, and then left, to follow the sign to Splatford and pass the Splatford Caravan Park. This is a quiet country lane heading for the distinctive tower of Lawrence Castle at the top of Haldon Hill. The road passes through a farmyard at Holloway Barton.

Turn left B to Chudleigh at Underdown Cross. The road takes you through the chestnut trees of Haldon Forest. There are

The River Exe at Exeter

plenty of places to park or picnic in these woods. The views on the left get more spectacular as the road climbs. **Turn right C at the next junction to head for the Bird of Prey Viewpoint on Buller's Hill.** This viewpoint overlooks a wide area of Haldon Forest. **Continue along this road past more car parks.**

As the road dips there is a little pets' cemetery on the right. Just beyond this is the so-called Lawrence Castle. It is, in fact, a belvedere, or memorial tower, built by Sir Robert Palk in 1788 as a monument to his friend, General Stringer Lawrence. The General left Palk his fortune of £50,000 enabling him to buy Haldon House. This vast mansion occupied a site lower down the hill. Most of it was demolished in 1920, apart from one wing which survives as a hotel. The tower is triangular and is supposed to be modelled upon Shrub Hill Tower in Windsor Great Park. It is almost hidden by trees planted shortly before work on the tower started.

Return to C and bear right at the crossroads. Descend through an avenue of old trees with mossy banks on either side. The entrance to Whiteway House, a mansion built in 1774 by the first Lord Boringdon and set in mature parkland, is on the right. **Go straight over the crossroads at Milestone Cross to pass over the A38 again and reach Chudleigh.**

When you come to the war memorial in the centre of the town turn right. Before the building of the modern highway, Chudleigh was on the main road between Exeter and Plymouth. Horses were changed here after the steep climb out of Exeter. It reached its zenith in 1841 when its innumerable inns and stables were busy with travellers. The coming of the railway severely dented trade, and the diversion of the main road took away the remainder of this passing trade. Much of the town was destroyed

SCALE 1:250 000 OR 1 INCH TO 4 MILES *1 CM TO 2.5 KM*

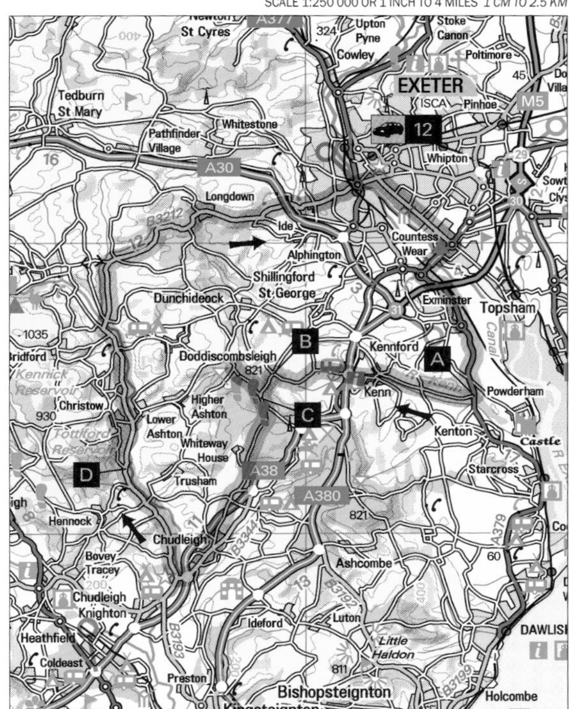

Canonteign Falls, claimed to be the highest waterfall in England

St Andrew's Church, Kenn

by fire in 1807, which accounts for its lack of buildings before this date. The Old Grammar School (1668) and the parish church are two exceptions. The fourteenth-century church, unusually, has a thirteenth-century tower. Unfortunately, it underwent a thorough Victorian restoration.

The B3344 takes you out of Chudleigh. Ugbrooke House and the picturesque Chudleigh Rocks (a large outcrop of limestone with old quarries and limekilns) are reached by a road to the left on the edge of the town. **The B3344 crosses the A38 and then meets the B3193. Turn right following the sign towards Canonteign Falls.** The road follows the valley past quarries and concrete works. These cease as the road reaches woodland. The river is close to the right. **Follow the sign off the main road to the left D to Canonteign Falls.** The country park entrance comes just before

• PLACES OF INTEREST •

Exeter's Historic Buildings
For information relating to the cathedral see page 70 and for a list of the city's attractions page 86.

The city began as a Roman outpost. The invaders halted their conquest here, leaving the Celtic tribes to their own devices. They built a walled town, known as Isca. Later, medieval town planners built their walls and gates on the Roman foundations. A walk of $1^1/2$ miles around the walls reveals the growth of the city through the ages.

The city was confined to the area within the walls until the eighteenth century when Exeter became a fashionable centre of culture, and the gentry built gracious brick terraces outside the medieval bounds as well as villas on the outskirts. Unhappily, much of Georgian Exeter was destroyed in the Baedeker air-raids of May 1942. The air-raids were thus called as the places attacked were supposed to have been randomly chosen from a guide-book.

Fortunately, the cathedral and most other ancient buildings were spared damage. However, a bomb did manage to penetrate the south choir aisle of the cathedral, and would undoubtedly have destroyed the medieval glass had it not previously been removed to a place of safety.

Like Norwich and York, Exeter had many medieval parish churches within the city walls. Only seven of the fifteen survive, all of them in cramped positions. Some have been converted to serve different uses. The best are St Mary Arches, now the diocesan library, St Martin's in the Cathedral Close, and St Mary Steps in West Street, originally the West Gate of the city.

Another feature of medieval Exeter was its intricate system of tunnels built to bring water into the walled city. Guided tours through sections of the tunnels start from an entrance in Princesshay.

The main Norman legacy, apart from the two towers of the cathedral, is Rougemont Castle. This was built by William the Conqueror in 1068 after his forces had quelled a rebellion by the citizens. Its most impressive feature is the gate tower which appears to have also served as the keep. The law courts, built in 1774, are surrounded by the remains of the inner bailey which was called upon to withstand a siege by King Stephen in 1136 (though the walls were more formidable at that time than they appear today).

The Guildhall is probably the city's most important building after the cathedral. It is a reminder that Exeter's first mayor was appointed in 1205. The present building occupies the site of a thirteenth-century guildhall and was built between 1468 and 1470. Its highly picturesque appearance from the High Street is the result of remodelling that took place between 1592 and 1593. It would have been even more extravagant when originally built as it was painted and gilded.

• PLACES OF INTEREST •

Haldon Forest
First planted in the 1920s it now comprises mature trees as well as others in earlier stages of growth. Haldon Hill is of green-sand, with thin soils ideal for forestry. In 1993 the whole of Haldon Forest became a Site of Special Scientific Interest. It is favoured by a wide variety of native and migratory birds of prey who soar above its windward slopes. Haldon is also a good intermediary feeding ground for birds en route to or from northern breeding grounds. Look for species such as red-footed falcon, black kite, marsh harrier, or Montagu's harrier, while rarities such as red-backed wood-chat, shrike and golden aureole can also be seen.

There is a butterfly walk suitable for the disabled.

Ugbrooke House and Park
The house was built in the late eighteenth century by Robert Adam, for the fourth Lord Clifford, who died in 1783. The beautiful parkland was landscaped by Capability Brown in the 1770s and is notable for 'Dryden's Seat', a grassy bank. Apparently, this was favoured by the poet, a frequent visitor to the earlier house (built by the first Lord Clifford who died in 1673). Dryden is supposed to have worked on his translation of Vergil at Ugbrooke.

The chapel dates from this era and has a startling, colourful interior in Italian Renaissance style. Remarkably, the house had declined and was being used as an agricultural store when it was rescued and restored in 1957. It contains fine furniture and paintings. Open mid-July– early September Tuesdays, Wednesdays, Thursdays and Sundays 1–5.30. Telephone: (01626) 852179.

Canonteign Falls
The Lady Exmouth Falls sheer drop of 220 feet (67 m) makes it the highest in England. There are also two other lesser, but still picturesque, cascades as well as lakes and woods on the private estate. The paths are steep in places, but Buzzard's View, at the top of Lady Exmouth Falls, provides a magnificent panorama and is well worth the effort. Open daily early March–mid-November 10–5.30. Sundays and school holidays in winter. Telephone: (01647) 52434.

---

the private entrance to Canonteign House, and both are on the left.

Continue along the road to pass a strange building with large windows. This was once the engine house of the Wheal Exmouth lead mine. Canonteign Barton, an enormous Tudor manor house, is just past this also on the right. The road was diverted to pass close behind the old building when Canonteign House was built to replace it in 1828. **The road meets a major road at Coombe Cross. Turn right to Ashton.** Pass a group of thatched cottages and descend the hill to the B3193 at Ashton. The ancient Spara Bridge carries the road into the village.

One of the painted figures on the rood-screen of St Michael's Church, Ashton

Cross the bridge if you wish to visit Ashton's magnificent parish church. This is a mile up the lane at Higher Ashton. Many consider it to be the best village church in Devon. It has beautifully-preserved, medieval woodwork and glass.

If you do not wish to see this church turn left on the B3193 towards Exeter. About 1/2 mile past Teign House Inn turn right off the main road to follow the B3193 across a pair of small bridges to reach a main road (B3212) a mile further on at Farrants Cross. Turn right here and climb up the hill to come into Longdown. From here there are good views towards Exeter as the road descends to pass beneath the A30 and then returns to the city. ■

• TOUR 13 •

IVYBRIDGE, SALTRAM HOUSE AND SHAUGH PRIOR

44 MILES – 2½ HOURS
START AND FINISH AT IVYBRIDGE

An appealing mix of coast and country, with the opportunity of visiting the grandest of Devon's stately homes, gives this tour continuous interest. It can easily be combined with a visit to Plymouth, and there are plenty of opportunities for walks on the clifftops, through woodland, or on the southern slopes of Dartmoor.

Take the B3211 out of Ivybridge to Ermington. Cross the A38 and then turn left to cross the bridge over the River Erme. After 2 miles the road enters Ermington past the church with its remarkable twisted spire. There is an elaborate, late-nineteenth-century lychgate leading into the churchyard. The church itself is gloriously decorated with animal woodcarvings, the work of the seven daughters of Edmund Pinwell, the rector who came to the church in 1880. Violet Pinwell later became a much sought-after wood-carver and established her own workshop in Plymouth. Her work can be seen in churches throughout the West Country.

When you come to the main road turn right towards Yealmpton. This road joins with the A379 at Hollowcombe Cross where you continue to head for Yealmpton. About a mile after this junction turn left A towards Holbeton and Mothecombe. Turn left again at the first junction to reach Ford. This is a charming hamlet with a narrow road twisting past pretty cottages.

The road arrives in Holbeton by the Mildmay Colours Inn. This takes its name from Lord Mildmay who, in 1878, rebuilt the great mansion of Flete, a mile to the north-east, and also restored the interior of the church. Like Ermington, the church here has a medieval spire (though this one is straight) which rises to a height of 113 feet (34 m). The interior is splendid, the restoration being sensitively carried out.

Turn left, pass the Dartmoor Union, and climb the hill out of the village. After 1 mile keep ahead when the lane joins a major road. This road runs along the coast. After 1 mile at Battisborough Cross you may like to turn left at a junction to Mothecombe where there is a car park almost at the end of the lane. Here the Coastal Path can be followed, either inland by the estuary or seawards along the cliffs.

At Stoke Cross B, about 3 miles further on, keep straight ahead towards Netton and Worswell to reach a car park for Stoke Point. From the car park a track leads to the open cliffs, and there is a steep initial descent to the coastal path. The going is then level, either westwards to Gara Point or eastwards to Stoke church. The church at Stoke Beach once served Newton and Noss. It stands close to the

Newton Ferrers is situated by the estuary of the River Yealm

SCALE 1:166 666 OR ABOUT 1 INCH TO 2½ MILES *1 CM TO 1.66 KM*

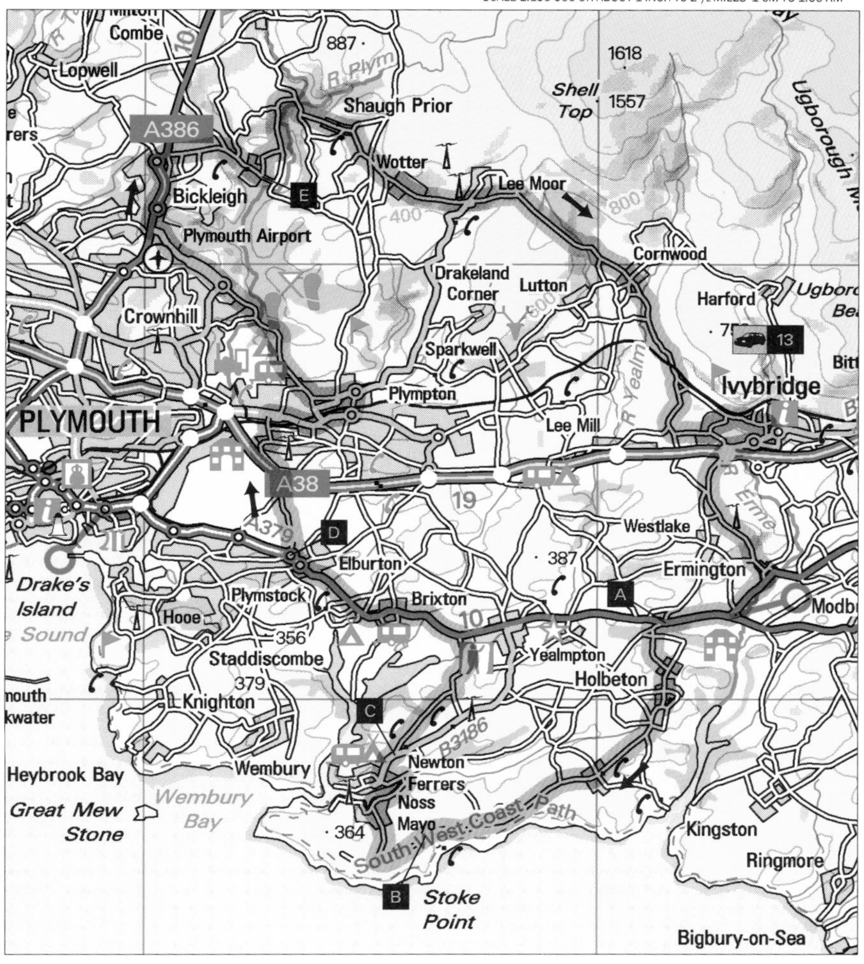

• PLACES OF INTEREST •

Ivybridge
The small town came into being after 1787 when the Stowford Paper Mills were established on the River Erme. Its water is particularly pure and soft, and therefore ideal for paper-making. Paper is still produced on this same site.

On the other side of the river there is a footpath which leads you through beautiful woodland to the eight-arched viaduct which takes the main line railway across the valley. The granite piers of Brunel's original viaduct (the supports and decking were of timber) can be seen by the side of the present one.

The construction of the trunk road has brought Ivybridge modern prosperity. Small businesses occupy purpose-built premises in industrial estates on the fringe of the town.

The Two Moors Way begins at Ivybridge and climbs up the flanks of Western Beacon, a splendid viewpoint for anyone with energy to spare.

Kitley Caves
Dramatically-lit stalactites and stalagmites, as well as other limestone formations, are to be seen in Kitley Caves. An interpretation centre explains these and shows some of the artefacts and remains found in the cave. It also illustrates the story of Sarah Martin who wrote the story of *Old Mother Hubbard* at Kitley nearly two hundred years ago.

A free leaflet explains the various delights of the riverside nature trail between the car park and the entrance to the caves. You might be lucky enough to see a kingfisher.

Open daily Easter–October 10–5. Telephone: (01752) 880885

shore and was abandoned in 1870, but has recently been rescued from ultimate decay by the Redundant Churches Fund. Very appropriately its dedication is to St Peter the Poor Fisherman.

Continue along the lane from the car park and turn right when the road ahead is shown to be a dead-end. There is another car park about a mile down this cul-de-sac. **Carry on and, at a T-junction, turn left into Noss Mayo.** The road descends into the village passing the church to the left and a turn down to the creekside. The church, built in 1882 to replace the one on the cliffs, has an opulent interior.

After the church the road descends to cross the creek at Bridgend. Turn sharply left here and follow the road which climbs up the opposite side of the river.

There has been a great deal of development in Newton Ferrers in the last thirty years and it is now difficult to see the views which once made the village so picturesque. However, there are still charming cottages by the shore, oak woods clothe the hillsides, and the River Yealm and the creek remain busy with pleasure craft. A seasonal passenger ferry crosses the Yealm to Warren Point, and from there it is a short but pleasant walk on the cliffs to Wembury. The village car park is at the top of the hill above the church, just off the green.

Take the B3186 out of Newton Ferrers towards Yealmpton. After about 1 mile turn left C on to a road signposted to Plymouth, only suitable for light vehicles. This road descends steeply, and there is a view to the left towards, what looks like, a doll's house in an idyllic setting. This is Kitley, Repton's remodelling of a Tudor house which was carried out in the 1820s for Edward Bastard.

Cross Puslinch Bridge over the River Yealm and pass the entrance on the right to Kitley Caves. **The road climbs up to the A379 on the outskirts of Yealmpton.** You can turn right here if you wish to visit the village and the Shire Horse Centre. **The tour continues by turning left to Brixton.** After Brixton you cross the Plymouth boundary. **Go straight over the first roundabout and turn to the right at the second D, following a sign to Plympton and Saltram House.** This road crosses over the A38 and, for a short distance, runs parallel to the trunk road before coming to the entrance to Saltram House on the left.

If you do not wish to visit Saltram carry on along this road and take the first turning to the left towards Plympton and the city centre. At the traffic lights turn right on to the B3416 into Plympton. Turn left at the roundabout which follows following a sign to Plym Bridge and

• *PLACES OF INTEREST* •

Saltram House

The rather plain appearance of the house, with its whiteness dazzling to the eyes, does not lead you to expect the richness of the interior. The house is especially important for its retention of many original furnishings and paintings. The latter were bought with the advice of Sir Joshua Reynolds, a friend of the Parker family, who lived close by, at Plympton. The Parkers bought the estate in 1712, and the house dates from the middle years of that century when the first John Parker began building himself a fine mansion. His son, another John, was the aesthete friend of Reynolds who employed Robert Adam to design new rooms, or redo the existing rooms. Few houses display Adam's work more splendidly.

Unfortunately, the succeeding generations of Parkers (by now Earls of Morley) failed to manage their fortune successfully, though from the time of the third Earl, who succeeded in 1884, they slowly recovered. In 1957 the house and estate came to the National Trust, and they have made it the showplace we find so enjoyable today.

Children will find the Great Kitchen and the pantries particularly interesting. The stables house not only carriages and historic cars, but a tramway locomotive. This reflects the investment which was a factor in the Parkers' disastrous change of fortune in the nineteenth century.

House open daily except Fridays and Saturdays April–October 12.30–5.30. Telephone: (01752) 336546.

Plym Bridge Woods

Not only are the woods a beautiful place to explore, they also illustrate many facets of the industrial activity which occupied the valley in the eighteenth and nineteenth centuries. At its peak, there were several slate quarries, a small mine producing silver and lead, three railway lines and a canal. To add to the complexity of this, there were water channels (leats) supplying the various water-wheels which powered the pumps, crushers and grinders essential for the industries.

A fascinating National Trust booklet explains all this. Currently priced £1, it is obtainable from: The Regional Information Office, Killerton House, Broadclyst, Exeter EX5 3LE.

Dartmoor Wildlife Park, Sparkwell, near Plymouth.

The park is proud of its breeding programme, its collection of big cats (including lions and tigers), and the fact that it has more than a thousand animals. It also has a falconry centre. Open every day of the year 10–dusk. Telephone: (01752) 837209.

Saltram House, a Georgian mansion with magnificently-furnished rooms

Boringdon Hall. Turn left at a second roundabout and cross over a little bridge as the road winds through the outskirts of Plympton. Keep on the main road when a road goes off to the right to Boringdon Hall. This was the home of the Parker family before they built Saltram House. The Tudor and seventeenth-century house was in decay until it was rebuilt as a hotel in 1986, much of the older work being restored.

The road descends to Plym Bridge, an eighteenth-century structure standing on the site of the original bridge, built in 1238. There is parking on the left, just before you go under a railway bridge. This was built for the South Devon and Tavistock Railway, but is now used as a cycle track. **Turn right, having crossed the river, and climb the lane up through woods.** The woods cease abruptly at the top of the hill when you reach an industrial estate. **Take the second exit at the roundabout towards the city centre and the Tavistock road. At the traffic lights turn right to join the A386. Keep on this road over two roundabouts and, 200 yards (183 m) after the second one at Roborough, turn right to Bickleigh and Shaugh Prior.** There is a fine view as you descend into the first of these villages.

Go past the army camps and, at the end of the one on the left, take the turning on the left E to Shaugh Prior. The church at Shaugh Prior can be seen on the hillside to the right. The road passes by a cycle way to the left, a continuation of the one at Plym Bridge. There is a view ahead of woods rising up to a rocky tor. This is Dewerstone Rock, which provides the best pitches for rock climbers in the area. There are parking places in the woods after a turn to Goodameavy goes off to the left. The road crosses the River Meavy over Shaugh Bridge. There are excellent riverside and woodland walks from here.

Shaugh Prior is a village notable for its attractive granite cottages. In the church there is a remarkable, medieval font cover. This was found in a cattle shed in 1871, and was painstakingly restored by its finder, the sculptor Harry Hems. Keep straight on through the village and pass over a cattle-grid to reach moorland. You can park here and take in a wonderful view over Plymouth.

At a staggered crossroads keep straight on towards Wotter. This village owes its existence to the china clay workings on the hill above it. The signboard of the Tramway Hotel shows a picture of an old locomotive once used in the industry. You may have seen this earlier at Saltram House. In fact, the tramway, as built by the South Devon and Tavistock Railway, was a disaster. A penalty clause in the contract meant that it was built shoddily, the viaduct at Wotter being built one bay short so that it was unsafe. It took much argument and expense before the line was completed to the owner's satisfaction, and the railway company never received payment for the original work. There have been extensive efforts to landscape the old spoil-heaps of the workings.

The road descends to beautiful woodland where there are several places to park and picnic. The area is called Newpark Waste and must be reclaimed land. The road narrows and is confined between stone walls as it approaches Cornwood. **Keep straight on through the village unless you wish to visit the Dartmoor Wildlife Park, in which case turn right at the pub.** After Cornwood, the road runs close to the main railway line before it bends right to pass beneath it and then twists round to reach the A38 and Ivybridge town centre. ■

The church at Shaugh Prior with its massive pinnacles

• TOUR 14 •

HONITON, COLYTON AND SIDMOUTH

30 MILES – 1½ HOURS
START AND FINISH AT HONITON

The countryside of East Devon, especially that away from the coast, is less frequently visited than Dartmoor or the lands to the west of the River Exe. This short tour serves as an appetiser for those new to the area. It meets the coast briefly at Sidmouth but, apart from this, stays inland, passing mainly through rich farming country. When the road climbs to the top of the sandy ridges which radiate from Honiton there are contrasting views of heath and woodland.

Head eastwards up the main street in Honiton, to pass the church on the left. At the top, move into the right-hand lane ready to turn on to the A35 signposted to Dorchester. The road crosses a railway and passes a charming castellated toll house on the right, known locally as Copper Castle. It has the original iron road gates.

As you climb the hill look to the right to see Bishop's Tower. This is an extraordinary building, 80 feet (24 m) high, built by Edward Coplestone, Bishop of Llandaff, in 1843. The bishop resided at Offwell House, and the tower was built to supply the house with running water, as well as to give employment to local people in hard times. He thought he would be able to see Llandaff from its battlemented top. Coplestones had lived in Offwell since Saxon times, and the Bishop Coplestone was the second in a long succession of Coplestones to be Vicar of Offwell. This family tradition began in 1773 and lasted until 1954. Offwell church has

• PLACES OF INTEREST •

Honiton
Honiton is well known for its book and antique shops, and on market days the main street is thronged with stalls.

William de Vernon, fifth earl of Devon, founded the first town here early in the thirteenth century. However, it probably had some importance long before this, being on the route of the Roman Fosse Way, which linked Leicester with Axmouth and Exeter.

Lace was probably introduced into the town by Flemish refugees during the reign of Elizabeth I. In 1699 there were 1,341 people employed in the industry in Honiton. During the eighteenth century fashion changed, and lace-making was also hit by the introduction of machinery to make net. Fortunately, there was another trade to fall back on. Honiton had pioneered the production of serge cloth in the eighteenth century, and this proved to be an equally successful industry.

Furthermore, the eighteenth century saw the beginning of the stagecoaches, and Honiton was strategically situated to benefit from this, being at the right distance from Exeter, at a point where various routes diverged.

Queen Victoria's use of Honiton lace in her wedding dress gave a short-lived boost to the industry and for a time demand exceeded supply. In the 1840s the fortunes of Honiton were at their peak. However, by the 1860s Honiton's fortunes had dwindled. Handmade lace was in decline again, lace was being made by machine in Nottingham, and the railway had replaced the stagecoach.

Honiton had other misfortunes. Like many other Devon towns it regularly suffered from disastrous fires. These swept through the thatched houses in 1672, 1747, 1754 and, worst of all, in 1765 when 115 houses were destroyed. Subsequent rebuilding explains the number of fine Georgian buildings in the town.

Townsfolk were finding it too irksome to climb to St Michael's Church, situated almost a mile out of the town on the slopes of the hill to the south-east, the site of the early village, and so, in 1835 St Paul's Church was built at the centre of the town. However, in 1911 fire also destroyed this church. Its beautiful rood-screen disappeared but, happily, many of the monuments survived, including the tomb of Thomas Marwood. He was physician to Elizabeth I, and saved the life of her favourite, the Earl of Essex, when all others had given him up for dead.

Sidmouth's shoreline from the coastal path

box pews and some good woodcarving.

Beyond Wilmington the countryside is typical of east Devon. Softly-moulded hills overlook red-earth farmland, meadows and tree-shaded hedges. **About 3 miles from Wilmington take the turn to the right A by a Little Chef which goes to Shute and Colyton.** Shute church will soon be seen by the imposing gatehouse to Shute Barton. The manor belongs to the National Trust and dates from 1380. It belonged to the Grey family in the fifteenth century. The estate came to the crown after the execution of Lady Jane Grey in 1476. If the house is closed, a good view of it can be had from the churchyard.

Continue on the road through pastoral countryside to Seaton Junction and the old station buildings. **Colyton can be seen to the right when you meet a main road just to the north of the town. Bear right down the hill and cross the bridge over the River Coly.** This takes you into the delightful little town with its wonderful church. Carry on through Colyton past an ornate street lamp decorated with the Prince of Wales' feathers. **Turn right just after this, up Hillhead, and bear left when the road forks, following the major road signposted to Seaton.** There is a picnic area and excellent viewpoint on the left B just after the junction.

Continue after the picnic place and keep on the major road when another to Colyford leaves to the left. At the T-junction turn right on to the A3052 and keep on the main road past turnings to Seaton and Beer (B3174). The latter junction is at Hangman's Stone, which is seen on the left. It is supposed to be haunted by the ghost of a pedlar. He stopped here to rest as his backpack was very heavy. He dozed off, fell from the stone, and was strangled by the straps of his pack.

About $\frac{1}{2}$ mile further on there is a monument to Dr Gilbert-Smith. The inscription says:

> *On this spot at half past nine o'clock after watching the glorious sunset of August 3 1904, Thomas Gilbert-Smith MD FRCS fell dead from his bicycle. Thunder and lightning immediately followed.*

Unfortunately, the bronze plaque showing his profile was stolen in 1981.

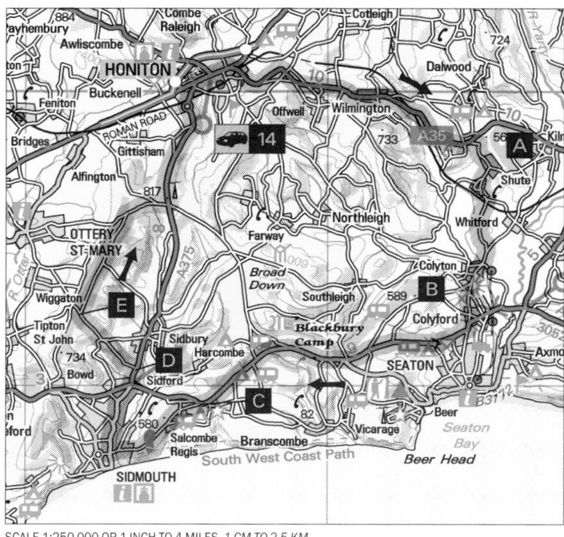

SCALE 1:250 000 OR 1 INCH TO 4 MILES *1 CM TO 2.5 KM*

Honiton is typical of the market towns of East Devon

Keep on the A3052 to pass the Three Horseshoes Inn and a turning to the right to Ottery St Mary. Two miles after this there is a turn on the left to the Donkey Sanctuary. About ½ mile further on take the road to the left C signposted to Salcombe Regis. Bear right when the road forks at the Salcombe Regis Thorn. A notice tells you that a thorn tree has been maintained here since Saxon times to act as a boundary marker.

Go straight on past the war memorial to reach the Norman Lockyer Observatory. There is a car park on the left here if you wish to walk along the beautiful paths leading to Salcombe Hill.

The road descends steeply after the car park through woodland. **Turn left at the bottom of the hill and cross the bridge. At a T-junction, in front of a cinema, turn right away from the centre of Sidmouth.** You are now on the B3175 which leads back to the A3052. **Turn right, and then left, to cross this and follow the A375 (Honiton road). After leaving the few houses behind take the first lane on the left D which is unsignposted, apart from a pointer to Burscombe Farm.** The narrow lane climbs steadily past Sidbury Castle, an early Iron Age hill-fort, on the right. When the road levels there is a view towards the sea. **Turn left at the first road junction and then keep on the major road, signposted to Ottery St Mary.** The road climbs steeply through woods.

At a road junction turn right E to East Hill Strips and Ottery St Mary. This road runs along the crest of the ridge of East Hill. There are numerous places to picnic, the official one being on the left at Long Whitecross. This road continues for nearly 3 miles before it reaches Chineway Head. **Turn right here to come to the Hare and Hounds Inn on the A375. Turn left to head back to Honiton.** The main road crosses Gittisham Hill where there are further places to park and picnic.

You may like to descend the steep lane to the left to Gittisham village, a lovely little place of thatched cottages. The church has an unspoilt, eighteenth-century interior with box pews. **The A375 finally comes to woodland and descends the hill to return to Honiton.** ■

The Tudor gatehouse at Shute

• PLACES OF INTEREST •

Shute

As you approach Shute from the north gigantic pilasters by the roadside warn of something out of the ordinary. Then you round a bend and see the dramatic silhouette of the gatehouse dwarfing that of the church beyond. It is a romantic scene almost impossible to catch with the camera, except under a dull sky when the lighting will be diffuse enough to illuminate the north-facing walls of the gatehouse, or, possibly, at 5.30 am on 21 June when sunlight may briefly rest on the battlemented facade. Although it may appear medieval, the gatehouse dates from c. 1580.

Shute Barton, the medieval manor house which stands just behind, is much older, dating from 1380. It is one of the most important medieval dwellings open to the public in Devon. It also has romance – it was the home of Lady Jane Grey before her execution in 1476. After this the property came to the Pole family. They made substantial additions and alterations in the sixteenth century. In 1787 Sir John William de la Pole built a new house on the hillside above Shute Barton. The medieval house fell into neglect, part of it being pulled down, and the remainder becoming a farmhouse. The National Trust took it over in 1959.

Open April–October Wednesdays and Saturdays 2–5.30. Telephone: (01297) 34692.

Colyton

The large church, with its eye-catching lantern, is the most obvious feature of the enchanting little town as you approach it from the north. Sometimes first impressions like this are followed by disappointment, but that can never be true in this case. It is easy to agree with Colyton's boast that it is the prettiest town in Devon. St Andrew's Church is delightfully light and airy. It dates from the thirteenth century, though the fifteenth-and sixteenth-century additions and alterations are more obvious. Its west window is one of the largest to be seen in any parish church. The Courtenay monument in the chancel is celebrated for the puzzle it offered students of heraldry. The tomb, despite the moving effigy, is not that of a child, but of the eighteen-year-old Margaret Beaufort, grand-daughter of John of Gaunt and wife of Thomas Courtenay, fifth Earl of Devon, who died in 1449.

There is a host of ancient buildings in the town, many dating from the fifteenth and

sixteenth centuries. Colyton's tannery, with its square chimney, is one of the last two surviving in the country to use the traditional oak bark process. It occupies its original eighteenth- and nineteenth-century buildings.

Sidmouth

For information see page 76.

The red cliffs of Sidmouth

• TOUR 15 •

EXETER, BICKLEIGH AND TIVERTON

40 MILES - 2½ HOURS
START AND FINISH AT EXETER

Exeter lies at the heart of Devon amidst delightful and varied countryside. The valleys of the River Exe and Culm have always been important routes and many beautiful towns and villages are sited along them. Ancient manor houses, like Fursdon, are hidden in folds of hills above the valleys, a treasured part of our history and architectural heritage. This drive takes you to many such secret places as well as to better-known attractions such as Bickleigh and Killerton.

From Exeter city centre take the A377 to Crediton, following the River Exe northwards. At the roundabout on the outskirts of the city, where the Crediton and Tiverton roads diverge, take the third exit and climb the hill. The road becomes narrow quite suddenly. Bear right A when it meets a major road at the top. A picnic place with a viewpoint over the city is immediately to the right.

Return to A and keep straight on to descend Stoke Hill. There is another extensive view over a patchwork of fields and the rich red soil of Devon. Picnic places can be found in the woodland on both sides of the road in Stoke Woods. There are also waymarked walks. **At the bottom of the hill the road rejoins the A396. Turn right into the village of Stoke Canon. Cross a causeway and two narrow bridges over the River Culm, to reach the village centre.** This river crossing, covering 800 feet (244 m), was in existence in 1326 when money for its upkeep

• PLACES OF INTEREST •

Exeter Cathedral

For details relating to Exeter's historic buildings see page 60 and the city's attractions page 86.

Exeter cathedral is one of the glories of the English Gothic style. A pair of Norman towers flank the richly-ornamented west front (the latter dating from 1329). The towers are all that remain of the original building, begun c. 1110. At this time William Warelwast, William the Conqueror's nephew, was bishop. It would have been interesting to have been an eavesdropper at chapter meetings when the idea of a new cathedral was discussed, c. 1260. Soon after, demolition and rebuilding began and continued until the end of the fourteenth century, interrupted briefly by the Black Death.

Visitors normally enter the cathedral from the west, and the view down the nave is breathtaking. Seven rows of columns lead up to the crossing beyond which is the rood-screen, by far the finest to be found in England, completed in 1324. Throughout the cathedral the vaulting is remarkable, both for its beauty and for its consistency, especially as work on it went on for almost a century, until its completion in 1369. During that time the five bishops and their masons resisted changing to more fashionable styles.

Visitors will find their own favourite features and details, but should look for the intricately-carved roof bosses, the thirteenth century misericords, and the medieval stained glass in the great east window.

Fursdon

There have been Fursdons at Fursdon since 1259, and it may be that there are pieces of their original house hidden in the fabric of the Georgian mansion. Certainly, traces of a medieval hall have been found in one of the regular bouts of remodelling. Displays in the house relate to events in the family's long history, including a costume exhibition which features clothes worn by them as far back as Georgian times.

Private footpaths lead through woodland up to Cadbury hill-fort, Iron Age defences once said to hold treasure guarded by a dragon! Open Easter–September Thursdays and Bank Holiday Mondays 2–4. Telephone: (01392) 860860.

SCALE 1:250 000 OR 1 INCH TO 4 MILES *1 CM TO 2.5 KM*

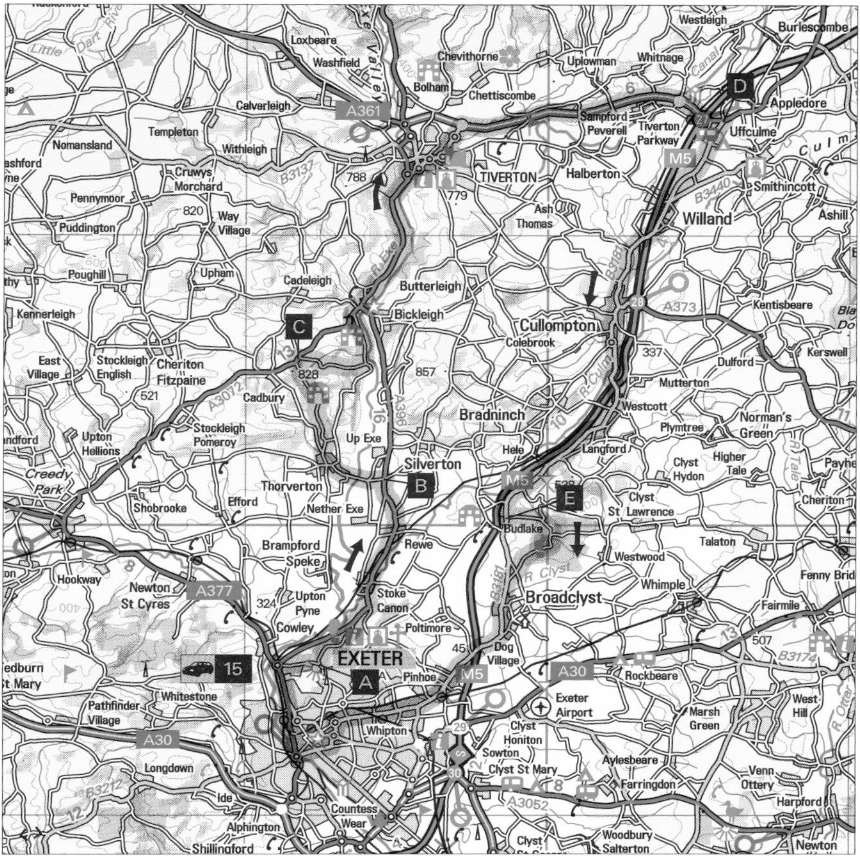

was left in a bequest. It was enlarged in the eighteenth and nineteenth centuries. The village had its share of disasters. The church was rebuilt in 1835 after being struck by lightning and, twelve years later, thirty buildings were destroyed when a spark from a locomotive set fire to the thatch of a cottage.

The next village is almost continuous with Stoke Canon and has the unusual name of Rewe. The attractive nineteenth-century estate cottages were built by W. H. Smith (founder of the newsagents and booksellers) when he owned the estate in 1895.

About 1½ miles from Rewe, just before the Ruffwell Inn, turn left B to Thorverton. Cross the River Exe to reach the village. Turn right at the Dolphin Inn to pass the church on the left. Thorverton was once famous for its building stone and its apricots, but both quarries and orchards are now defunct.

Follow the signs to Fursdon through beautiful countryside. There are soon views to the right over a deep valley. Fursdon House can be seen quite well from the lane and is open to the public. Visitors to the house are allowed to use private footpaths to reach Cadbury Castle, an Iron Age fort, to the left of this lane, before it reaches the A3072.

The west front of Exeter cathedral

If you wish to see Cadbury Castle without visiting Fursdon, turn left onto the A3072 and then left again to pass Cadbury church. You will reach a footpath which climbs to the top of the hill from the left of the road. The reward is a fabulous view which extends from Exmoor to Dartmoor. On a good day the Quantocks and Bodmin Moor are also visible.

Turn right on to the A3072 and then, in a short distance, turn right C opposite an Animal Welfare Centre down a lane signposted to Chilton. This is a narrow lane which winds through farmyards gradually descending into the valley of the River Exe. Turn left at the T-junction by the river and follow the lane past Bickleigh Castle. The castle proves to be a wonderful surprise – an ancient gatehouse and keep joined to a thatched farmhouse. The equally appealing thatched chapel, which dates from Norman times, is to the right of the lane. **The lane rejoins the A3072 just above Bickleigh Bridge. Cross the first of the bridges (over the River Dart of mid-Devon) and then turn left on to the A396.** However, at this point you may like to cross the other bridge over the River Exe to visit Devonshire's Centre at Bickleigh Mill.

Tiverton Castle

The A396 follows the river upstream through a beautiful valley to reach Tiverton. **Go straight over the first roundabout and turn right at the second following the 'other routes' signs. This takes you on to Great Western Way and across the river. Head for the M5 over four more roundabouts and cross the A361 before joining it. Cross over the motorway on to the A38 and pass a Little Chef. After 1/4 mile, at the Old Cottage Inn, turn right D on to the B3181 towards Willand and Uffculme.** The B3440 soon goes off to the left to Uffculme and the Working Wool Museum. Willand is a village divided by motorway, railway and main road.

Remain on the B3181 after the village to pass the entrance to Verbeer Manor Country Park. Continue along the main road through Cullompton. One of Devon's outstanding parish churches can be found here. The main street, like many others in the county, was frequently destroyed by fire (the town lost 264 houses in 1838). The street is broad at first, but soon becomes narrow. The

The thatched farmhouse seen from the castle gatehouse at Bickleigh

broad section served as a cattle market until the 1920s. In the eighteenth century it was the venue for bull-baiting, which gave it its name, Higher Bullring. At the Manor House Hotel the road becomes Fore Street and is comparatively narrow.

Turn left at the roundabout at the end of the town by Toad Hall and stay on the B3181 to cross the motorway again. The road follows the motorway closely for the next 4 miles.

If you wish to visit Killerton turn right at Beare, on a road which crosses the motorway, signposted to Silverton Mill. **Otherwise, keep on the B3181 to the next junction at Budlake and turn left E to Caddihoe and Ashclyst Forest.** This is a quiet country lane passing thatched cottages typical of this part of mid-Devon. There are parking places and picnic sites in the forest.

Keep on the main road heading towards Broadclyst to pass Forest Gate car park on the left. When the woods end the road descends and gives views over arable countryside.

Go straight over a cross-roads and then turn left on to the B3181. The road twists its way into Broadclyst, now mainly the property of the National Trust. It has a chronicled history going back to 1001, when the village was burned by the Danes. The Red Lion Inn is one of several beautiful buildings grouped around the church on the green. The church has a fine tall tower. Inside is a monument to Sir John Acland, the first Acland to live in the parish, who died in 1620. The Aclands were great benefactors of the village, culminating in their gift of the Killerton estate to the National Trust during 1942 and 1943.

From Broadclyst the B3181 crosses the motorway and comes to Pinhoe on the outskirts of Exeter. **From here follow the signs back to the city centre.** ■

• *PLACES OF INTEREST* •

Bickleigh
The village is on the east side of the river and the castle on the west. The two are linked by a graceful bridge making it one of Devon's most famous beauty spots. The castle is a fascinating building, a picturesque jumble of medieval fortress and charming thatched cottages. The gatehouse is the most impressive remnant of the fortified manor house, and probably dates from the fifteenth century when a branch of the Courtenay family moved here. They were succeeded by the Carews in the following century. The buildings were badly damaged in the Civil War and the gatehouse was originally considerably taller. On the other side of the road is a thatched chapel claimed to be the oldest complete building in Devon, dating from the eleventh century.

Bickleigh Castle. Open Easter–Spring Bank Holiday Wednesdays, Sundays and Bank Holidays 2–5.30. Spring Bank Holiday–early October daily except Saturdays 2–5.30. Telephone: (01884) 855363.

Devonshire's Centre, Bickleigh Mill. A complex which combines craft workshops with interesting exhibitions illustrating the working of a nineteenth-century farm complete with shire horses. There is also a motor museum and narrow gauge railway. Restaurant and gift shop. Open daily Easter–Christmas weekends. January–Easter from 10. Telephone: (01884) 855419.

Cold Harbour Mill Working Wool Museum, Uffculme
Throughout history the prosperity of Devon depended on the wool trade. Cold Harbour Mill is a working museum which has manufactured woollens for almost two hundred years. Visitors can watch every stage in the process of producing cloth and yarn. At certain times the steam engine which once powered the mill can be seen working. Open daily April–October 11–5. Telephone: (01884) 840960 for other times.

Killerton
The house dates from 1778 and was the home of the Acland family until 1944. Its furnishings reflect the history of the house, the rooms displaying the costumes of the era, from eighteenth century to the present day. They are from the Paulise de Bush costume collection. The fifteen-acre garden was partly land-scaped by William Robinson. Though famous for its rhodo-dendrons it is beautiful throughout the year.

Park and garden open daily 10.30–dusk. Killerton House open April–October daily except Tuesdays 10–5.30. Telephone: (01392) 881345.

Tiverton's splendid church stands next to the castle

• TOUR 16 •

EXMOUTH AND THE COAST OF EAST DEVON

71 MILES – 3 HOURS
START AND FINISH AT EXMOUTH

Allow plenty of time for this drive. It is crammed with so much of interest it could easily take up the whole day! The first part follows the coast eastwards, often using byways rather than the main roads. There are plenty of places where you can walk along the cliffs or explore towns like Sidmouth and Lyme Regis. The return is via Honiton and Ottery St Mary, where the church is thought by many to be the best in Devon after Exeter cathedral.

From Exmouth Station head through the town, following the signs for Budleigh Salterton. Pass Holy Trinity Church to the right and then turn left at the roundabout that follows on to the B3178. The World of Country Life is reached by a road to the right, which also goes to Sandy Bay. After this the road leaves the town, passing through a pine wood to come to a roundabout.

Turn right here, keeping on the B3178. Cross a disused railway to come into the village of Knowle. Stay on the main road when the B3178 leaves on the left to Bicton Park. Continue on this road through Budleigh Salterton. You have a brief view of the seafront, the location of Millais' painting *The Boyhood of Raleigh*. The road heads northwards to East Budleigh.

As you come up to a cross-roads you will see an obelisk in the distance. This was erected in 1730 to serve as an eye-catcher when viewed from Bicton House. Also of interest is the brick pillar to the right of the road. This was erected in 1580 by the Sheriff of Devon on whose orders a witch was burned at the crossroads.

Turn right at this crossroads if you wish to visit Otterton Mill. The water-mill has ground corn since the time of the Domesday Book. **Otherwise keep straight on. Pass the entrance to Bicton Park A and then the grand gateway to Bicton College of Agriculture both on the left.**

• PLACES OF INTEREST •

Exmouth
The town was Devon's first resort. In the eighteenth century it developed from a 'fishing townlet' to a place favoured by people of fashion, both for holidays and permanent residences. Lady Nelson and Lady Byron both spent time here when their husbands were unable to be with them. Exmouth's popularity continued until the mid-nineteenth century, when it began to be eclipsed by Torquay.

Once the railway reached Exmouth in 1861 its sandy beaches began to attract a different clientele and, until the Second World War, it was a typical family resort. Today, it serves more as a dormitory to Exeter, but has also adapted to please modern holidaymakers.

World of Country Life, Sandy Bay. Working agricultural museum. Open daily Easter–October 10–6. Telephone: (01395) 274533.

A la Ronde, Summer Lane. A unique sixteen-sided house built in 1796 for two spinsters. Now a National Trust property. Bizarre interior includes a shell room and another with a frieze of feathers. Telephone: (01395) 265514.

SCALE 1:250 000 OR 1 INCH TO 4 MILES *1 CM TO 2.5 KM*

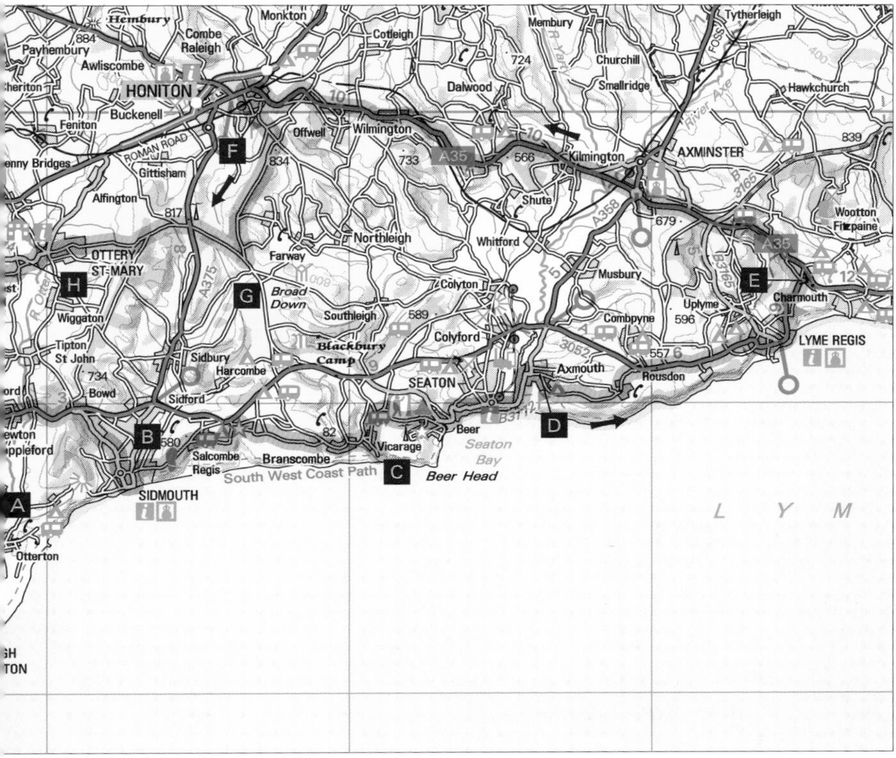

Carry on through Colaton Raleigh passing the Otter pub on the right. The next village is Newton Poppleford where you turn right on to the A3052 following the sign towards Lyme Regis. Cross the River Otter and climb a steep hill. A parking place on the left, just beyond the summit, provides a wonderful view.

After this, opposite the ancient Bowd Inn, turn right to Sidmouth on to the B3176. However, if there has been recent heavy rain, or you do not wish to negotiate a rather long ford, continue along the main road and take the next turn to the right. This will take you down to Sidmouth, passing through Woolbrook, to join the B3175. You will eventually come to the Radway Cinema on the right. Turn left here. When you pass the toll house continue to follow the tour as instructed after B below.

The B3176 takes you directly down to Sidmouth's beautiful seafront. Turn left along the Esplanade. Most of the buildings here, now guest-houses, were originally built as private houses. **Turn left at the Inshore Lifeboat House to pass the swimming pool and the Tourist Information Centre (TIC). Go down York Street, pass the Swan Inn and then bear right into Riverside Road to come to the ford. Cross this to come out facing a charming little toll house and turn right B.**

Turn right off the Seaton road to climb up Salcombe Hill Road towards the Observatory. The climb is long and steep and takes you through beautiful woodland. At the top you will see a National Trust car park on the right, opposite the Norman Lockyer Observatory. Footpaths lead through the woods to join other paths on the clifftop.

Continue along the road and turn right at the war

Branscombe village

memorial to descend the hill into Salcombe Regis. A footpath to the beach leaves on the right. **Turn sharply to the right just after the church. The lane climbs steeply to pass the Dunscombe Manor Caravan Park and then bears left to pass the Donkey Sanctuary.** This is open every day throughout the year.

After the sanctuary take the turn on the right to Weston and Branscombe. After 200 yards (183 m) turn right again on to a lane signposted to the Stoneleigh Holiday and Leisure Centre. At a T-junction turn right into Weston. Keep straight on to Street and Branscombe after a road goes off to the left. This is a narrow lane with few passing places. The descent into Street is steep. **Turn right at a T-junction and follow the wooded valley.** This takes you down to Branscombe. The church is dedicated to St Winifred, an obscure Celtic saint, and work from Norman times onwards can be seen here. There is a car park after the thatched smithy.

Follow the lane towards Beer to pass the Mason's Arms Hotel, where a lane goes down to the beach at Branscombe Mouth C. There is another car park here. **From the car park climb the hill back to the village, but fork right when the lane divides to**

• PLACES OF INTEREST •

Otterton Mill
A water-mill has operated here for a thousand years. Museum, craft workshops etc. Open daily Easter–October 10.30–5.30 (11.30–4.30 November–Easter). Telephone: (01395) 568521.

Bicton Park and Gardens
Over fifty acres of magnificent gardens are the centre-piece of the park. Although the garden was laid out to a Le Nôtre design c. 1735, it was considerably altered by the Rolles in the nineteenth century. The excavation of the lake took place in 1812 and was carried out by French prisoners of war. Later, an arboretum and pinetum were planted and, c.1830, the palm house was built.

Open daily March–October 10–6. Telephone: (01395) 568465.

Sidmouth
Sidmouth is the genteel resort par excellence. Its situation attracted gentlefolk in the early nineteenth century when the Napoleonic wars prevented them from travelling in Europe. Many people built themselves 'cottages' (we would call them mansions) in choice positions overlooking the sea. Later, fine Georgian terraces were built closer to the sea. The promenade was built soon after Queen Victoria came to the throne. As a child she had spent a winter at Sidmouth with her parents, the Duke and Duchess of York.

Sidmouth's pebbly beach was one of the reasons why the resort failed to appeal to families, but this did not detract from its popularity with an older generation.

The Vintage Toy and Train Museum, Field's Department Store, Market Place. Comprehensive collection of model railways of days gone by. Die-cast and tin-plate toy models. Open daily except Sundays and Bank Holidays Easter–October 10–5. Telephone: (01395) 515124.

Seaton Tramway
The three-mile-long tramway runs from Seaford to near Colyton. It follows the west bank of the beautiful River Axe. Services daily Easter–September Monday–Friday in October. Telephone: (01297) 21702.

Beer
The tiny, and very pretty, fishing port shelters beneath a massive cliff which rises to a height of 426 feet (130 m). It is the first of the succession of chalk headlands encountered by ships as they sail up the English Channel. The famous quarries here supplied stone for many great buildings like Westminster Abbey and St Paul's Cathedral. Most of East Devon's beautiful churches also use Beer stone. The public are able to explore its underground passages which lead to enormous caverns.

Beer Quarry Caves. Open daily Easter–October 10–5.30 (but 11–4 in October). Telephone: (01297) 20986.

Pecorama Pleasure Gardens. The ultimate for the model railway enthusiast. All sorts of model railways, up to a 7¼-inch passenger-carrying railway. Open Monday–Friday Easter–October 10–5.30 and Saturday 10–1. Telephone: (01297) 21542.

Ottery St Mary
The glory of the pleasant little town is its church, founded in 1342 by Bishop John de Grandisson of Exeter, as a college for secular priests. The bishop modelled it on his own cathedral. It has beautiful vaulting and colourful ceiling bosses, outstanding medieval woodwork including the reredos and an eagle lectern, and interesting monuments.

Cadhay (1 mile north-west of Ottery) is a beautiful Tudor house concealed behind a Georgian front. An unusual feature is the internal courtyard with statues of Henry VIII and his three children (the date 1617 is carved beneath the figure of Elizabeth). Open July–August Tuesdays–Thursdays, Sundays and Mondays of late spring and late summer Bank Holidays 2–5.30. Telephone: (01404) 812432.

rejoin the road to Beer. On the left a lane goes to Bovey House Hotel, said to have sheltered King Charles. On the right there is an entrance to Beer Old Quarry, and, a little further on a road on the right leads to the Pecorama Pleasure Gardens.

A major road on the right drops down into the fishing village of Beer, but the tour continues by going ahead to join the B3174, signposted to Seaton. Follow the main road to Seaton seafront, joining a one-way system which leads to a roundabout. Go left here, following the sign to Lyme Regis, and then straight over the mini-roundabout. The terminus of the tramway is to the left. Cross the bridge over the River Axe. The road then follows the eastern bank of the river.

Continue to Axmouth and, just past the Ship Inn, take the turning right D into Chapel Street. Pass the post office and then turn right again up Stepps Lane. This little country lane climbs up steeply. There are footpaths on the right which lead to the coast path on Dowlands Cliffs.

At a junction go straight on following the sign to Rousdon. When you meet the A3052 at the Dower House Hotel turn right. This road takes you into Dorset and to Lyme Regis. You can see Lyme Bay as you come into the town, with Golden Cap, the flat-topped hill, in the distance. The round, thatched house, seen as you descend the hill, is Umbrella Cottage. There is a parking place to the right, opposite a turning to the left to Uplyme and Axminster. Lyme Regis is one of the most picturesque seaside towns on the south coast.

Follow the main road through the narrow streets of Lyme Regis and out towards Charmouth. After about 2 miles take the minor road to the left E to Axminster

The magnificent parish church at Ottery St Mary

and then bear left again. This road descends steeply. **When you reach the A35 turn left to Honiton and Axminster, crossing the county border just before Raymond's Hill.** Pass the Hunter's Lodge Hotel and, if you wish to visit the old town of Axminster, take the right turn. **Otherwise, keep on the A35 to cross bridges over the River Axe and then the River Yarty.** The main road runs through delightful countryside to reach Honiton.

Enter the town through its toll gates. At the roundabout take the first exit which leads into the centre. Turn left at Lloyds Bank, about halfway up the main street, into New Street. Continue past the station and, opposite a church at a mini-roundabout, turn left F. Follow the signs to Northleigh and Seaton. The road climbs steeply to a golf club. **Turn right towards Farway and Seaton.** This is a high road following one of the sandy ridges radiating from Honiton. **Continue until you come to a main road and turn right G. Go straight over the A375 at the crossroads at Putts Corner, by the Hare and Hounds pub.** A turn to the left goes to White Cross Picnic Place. **Stay on the main road which dips down after this.**

Carry on through Ottery St Mary, keeping straight on at Moira's Tea Shop to join the one-way system. At the end of this turn left (the road to the right goes to Cadhay House) and cross the bridge over the River Otter. Then take the first turn left H into Strawberry Lane, following the sign to West Hill. Stay on this road which becomes quite narrow. Just after passing a garage on the right, leave the main road to the right, following the sign to Exeter. This road skirts West Hill and comes to the B3180 at crossroads at Rockbeare Hill. Turn left here to Exmouth. When, after nearly 3 miles, you come to the Half Way Inn and the A3052, turn left and then immediately right to cross it, continuing on the B3180. There are parking and picnic places.

At Four Firs Cross keep straight on. Turn right when the road forks, to head to Lympstone and Exmouth. The National Trust's house, A la Ronde, is to the right as you come to the Exmouth town sign. Lyme Bay is spread out in front of you as you approach the town. ■

Beer is a delightful seaside village

• TOUR 17 •

BOVEY TRACEY, FERNWORTHY RESERVOIR AND DARTMEET

50 MILES – 2½ HOURS
START AND FINISH AT BOVEY TRACEY

This route follows narrow lanes, particularly around Lustleigh, and there are also steep gradients. Lustleigh Cleave is a very picturesque area, immensely popular with the Victorians. The Fernworthy Reservoir is a more recent beauty spot dating from 1942. The tour visits Dartmeet and Widecombe before returning to Bovey Tracey via Haytor.

Take the B3387 out of Bovey Tracey passing the Dartmoor Inn on your left. Continue past Parke (where the National Park has its headquarters) and then fork right on to the major road towards Manaton and Becka Falls. The road narrows quite suddenly and becomes a single track as it climbs steadily. After about a mile a road to Haytor goes off to the left and, about ¼ mile beyond this, as the road twists round to the left, there is a white house ahead. **Take the turn to the right A by the white house.** This narrow, unsignposted road winds through woodland with an abundance of sweet chestnut trees. There are parking spaces by a bridge over the River Bovey. **After the bridge bear right to Lustleigh. Cross another bridge, this one tiny and humpbacked, and pass under the disused railway. Keep heading for Lustleigh by bearing left at the next junction.** Just after this there is a wonderful view of the village in its steep valley. **Turn left when you meet the road from Moretonhampstead to reach the village centre.**

Bear left when a road goes off to Caseley, and follow the road round to the left into Lustleigh. The church is to the right and the Cleave Hotel to the left. **Turn left at the post office towards Rudge and keep ahead as the road narrows and climbs steadily. When you come to the T-junction on a very steep incline at Rudge Cross turn right towards North Bovey.**

Lustleigh Cleave, a steep valley caused partly by earth movement and partly by the eroding power of the River Bovey, is over the ridge to the left. There are one or two parking spaces. Footpaths lead off both sides of the road,

• PLACES OF INTEREST •

Bovey Tracey
The second part of the town's name remembers Henry de Tracey, its founder in the early thirteenth century. His forefather was Sir William Tracey, one of the knights who murdered Thomas à Becket in Canterbury cathedral in 1170. Later, in recompense, he built the parish church with its lengthy dedication is to Saints Peter, Paul, and Thomas of Canterbury. The church is situated above the town and overlooks Dartmoor. Its finest features are the tall, slender tower, the rood-screen which dates from 1427, and the stone pulpit of much the same date.

Bovey (pronounced 'Buvvy') became a busy market town depending on the wool trade in medieval times. However, it was also able to rely on the mining of lignite and on the deposits of ball clay which led to a pottery industry. Bovey's position is close to an ancient lake, which silted up aeons ago, when beds of both materials were laid down. The geology of the district also resulted in a brickworks being sited near the town.

The old railway line to Moretonhampstead, opened in 1866, provides a pleasant walk for a mile or so northwards out of the town. It gives a sample of the delightful scenery which would have been enjoyed from the line until it finally closed in 1964, in spite of attempts to preserve it.

The House of Marbles and Teign Valley Glass. The unique factory occupies the site of the old pottery at Bovey Tracey. It displays the biggest range of marbles (round ones) in the world. There is a museum area. Visitors can watch glass blowing. Open Monday–Saturday 9–5 (and Sundays Easter–September). Telephone: (01626) 835358.

Parke Rare Breeds Farm
For information see page 14.

those to the left leading to the top of the Cleave. Driving along this lane requires a lot of care, but you may be able to pause to enjoy the vistas to the right.

Turn left at Sandurck Cross to North Bovey and then, after about ½ mile, turn left again B following the sign to Manaton. There are more lovely views from this road. **Go over a pair of pack-horse bridges to cross the River Bovey again. Ignore the lane signposted to Manaton on the left and, at a T-junction turn left, again heading towards Manaton. At the next junction at Langstone Cross turn right to follow the signpost to Hound Tor, Widecombe and Moretonhampstead. Then at the crossroads at Heatree Cross turn right on to the road signposted to Moreton-hampstead and Chagford. After 2 miles turn left on to the B3212 at Watching Place. After ¼ mile, turn right off the main road to Lettaford and again right when the road forks towards Fernworthy and Chagford.** Cross a lovely bridge where there is a delightful place to picnic by the stream. **Go past a turn to the right soon after the bridge and straight over a tiny crossroads.**

Dartmeet is a favourite playground for children

Take the turning left C at Corndon Cross (its signpost is hidden in the bank to the right of the road and is easily missed) heading towards Corndon and Hurston. At a second Corndon Cross follow the road round to the right to Fernworthy Reservoir. At the next T-junction turn left following signs to the reservoir to reach the open moor. Go over a cattle-grid into the Forestry Commission land. There are prehistoric hut circles just before the official car park and picnic place.

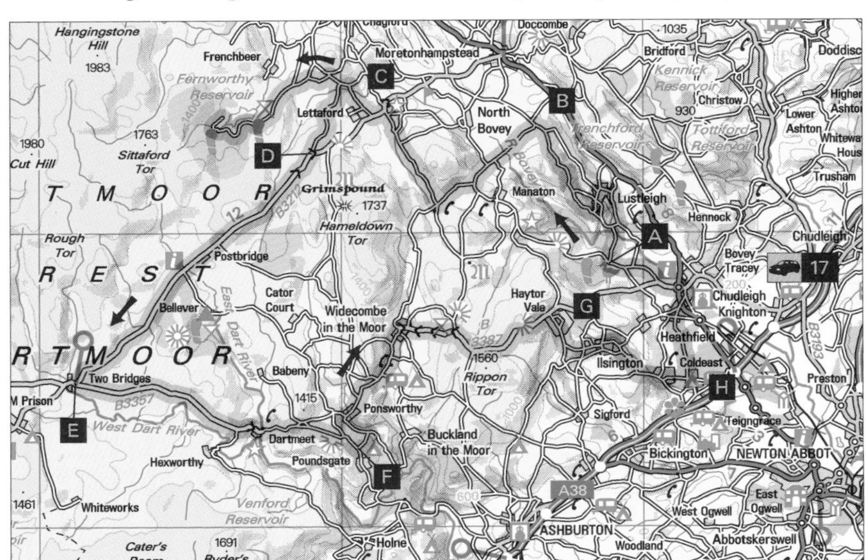

SCALE 1:250 000 OR 1 INCH TO 4 MILES *1 CM TO 2.5 KM*

Fernworthy Reservoir provides good fishing

Return by the same road to C and turn right. At the next crossroads bear right to Jurston. There is an open farmyard and, after this, the little lane climbs to the moor. There is a good view of Shapley Tor and Challacombe Down from here.

When you reach the B3212 at Jurston Cross turn right D to Postbridge and Princetown. Pass the Warren Inn, one of the famous Dartmoor hostelries built to help quench the thirst of tin miners. Many people stop at Postbridge to photograph friends and relatives on the famous clapper bridge. There is a National Park Information Centre in the car park. Footpaths lead to many of Dartmoor's most remote beauty spots with evocative names like Laughter Hole and Crock of Gold.

Continue on the B3212. When the trees end to the left and the road dips to a bridge, you will see the Powder Mills to the right. Some of the cottages are now occupied by a pottery.

Pass Cherrybrook Hotel to meet the B3357 and turn left E to Dartmeet and Ashburton. This is a barren stretch of moorland with views to the left over the East Dart River. **Go past the turn to the right to Hexworthy.** Pass the home of the Dartmoor pixie, to the left just before Brimpts Farm. Cross the bridge at Dartmeet, a famous beauty spot. Children love to scramble over the boulders and splash in the East Dart River. This river joins with the West Dart just below the bridge to make the River Dart. The ancient clapper bridge at Dartmeet was used until 4 August 1826 when a terrible thunderstorm swept it away. Although it was repaired towards the end of the century another storm left it in the condition we see it today.

The road climbs up between Sharp Tor to the right and Corndon Tor to the left. **Go past the turn to the left to Sherril and Babeny.** About a mile further on there is a fine view southwards from Bel Tor. **Then, opposite an unpretentious Methodist church at Poundsgate, take the turning left F which leads to Leusdon. Keep left at Leusdon where a modern monolith commemorating the Queen's Jubilee stands on the small triangle of green.** This road leads past Forder Bridge (the cluster of houses to the left), crosses the West Webburn River over a bridge which dates from 1666, and then climbs the hill past Ponsworthy's post office.

Keep on the main road past several turnings to reach Widecombe. Drive through the village and then climb the

This view of North Bovey can be seen from near Sanduck Cross

hill out of Widecombe on the B3387. It is worth stopping in one of the car parks near the top of the hill to take in the view back to Widecombe. The numerous car parks here make access to the moor very easy. If you wish to climb Haytor Rocks use one of the car parks before the road begins to descend, unless you want some strenuous exercise! On a good day the view from the top is fantastic.

Just after Moorland Crafts on the right turn right G into Haytor Vale. Ignore the turn which follows immediately to the left, which snakes through the village, and carry on the major road past the Ilsington Hotel to Ilsington church. This dates from the thirteenth century and was enlarged in the late-fifteenth. John Ford, the dramatist, was baptised here in 1586. **Follow the road round to the left past the church, towards Liverton and Newton Abbot. The road drops quite steeply through woods and comes to Liverton. Pass through this village and, at Cummings Cross H turn left towards Bovey Tracey. Keep on this road and go straight over the next crossroads to cross a bridge over the A382 to return to the town.** ■

Lustleigh is beautifully situated in a fold of the hills

• PLACES OF INTEREST •

Lustleigh

This is a picture-postcard village at the heart of magnificent scenery, once described as 'Devonia's Alps'. It is not quite so renowned today, perhaps for the prosaic reason that there is little car parking available. At the height of its popularity, at the turn of the century, excursionists flocked to Lustleigh by train to visit Lustleigh Cleave, a dramatic gorge with the River Bovey running through it. In those days the Cleave was grassy. Since then scrubby trees and undergrowth have covered the grass. Nevertheless, it provides excellent walking, and several footpaths run through and above it. On Sharpitor, at the southern end of the Cleave, there used to be an enormous boulder, perfectly balanced, which would rock just enough to crack a hazel nut. Vandals sent it crashing down into the Cleave in 1951. It is still marked on Landranger maps as the Nutcracker. Not unnaturally, for such a romantic place, the Cleave has its ghost story. In the year 1240 the King ordered the Sheriff of Devon and twelve of his knights to 'perambulate' his Royal Forest of Dartmoor in order to assert its boundaries. This stately cavalcade is supposed to be re-enacted, passing through the Cleave with banners flying and spurs and harnesses tinkling.

Fernworthy Reservoir

Dartmoor's water is exceptionally pure and wholesome, as well as being comparatively plentiful. It is not surprising, then, that substantial amounts are used for drinking-water supplies. Fernworthy Reservoir helps to supply the needs of Torbay. It dates from 1936 though, owing to the outbreak of war and other unforeseen difficulties, it did not become operational until 1942.

The reservoir covers seventy-six acres and is surrounded by forestry planted in the 1920s. It has become a fine habitat for a wide variety of birds, and its south-western shore is a Special Protection Zone. The reservoir is stocked with brown trout which provide good sport for fly fishing.

The Powder Mills

This remote spot was ideal for the making of gunpowder, an industry which flourished here from 1844 until 1890, employing one hundred men. It seems to have been a very hit-and-miss factory, batches of the powder being tested by firing a cannon-ball from a mortar. The gunpowder was graded depending on how far the ball carried. Charcoal, sulphur and saltpetre were ground between great millstones powered by the stream, the Cherry Brook. They were then mixed together, sometimes with disastrous results. An explosion in 1857 caused £500 of damage, though there is no mention of death or injury. However, one theory explaining the local supernatural phenomenon, the 'Hairy Hands', suggests that it was caused by a disaster down at the mill. The Hairy Hands are supposed to pull cars off the road as they travel between Postbridge and Two Bridges. The Powder Mills closed in the 1890s when the invention of dynamite made gunpowder obsolete.

• TOUR 18 •

PRINCETOWN, MORETONHAMPSTEAD AND TAVISTOCK

54 MILES – 2½ HOURS
START AND FINISH AT PRINCETOWN

This route keeps to main roads and both driving and navigation should prove easy. It passes through some of the best Dartmoor scenery. You will visit Okehampton, with its formidable castle, and Tavistock, notable for the influence exerted on it by a powerful medieval abbey and by a mining bonanza in the nineteenth century.

From Princetown take the B3212 to Two Bridges and Moretonhampstead. Cross the cattle-grid on to the open moor and bear right on to the B3357 towards Dartmeet and Moretonhampstead. At Two Bridges the road crosses the West Dart River. The old bridge to the right is the turnpike bridge built in 1792. Parking places can be found where the footpath to Wistman's Wood leaves to the left. The walk to the wood will give you a taste of Dartmoor's beauty.

Bear left when the road divides A taking the B3212 towards Moretonhampstead. A famous stretch of Dartmoor countryside follows. Bellever Tor can be clearly seen to the right

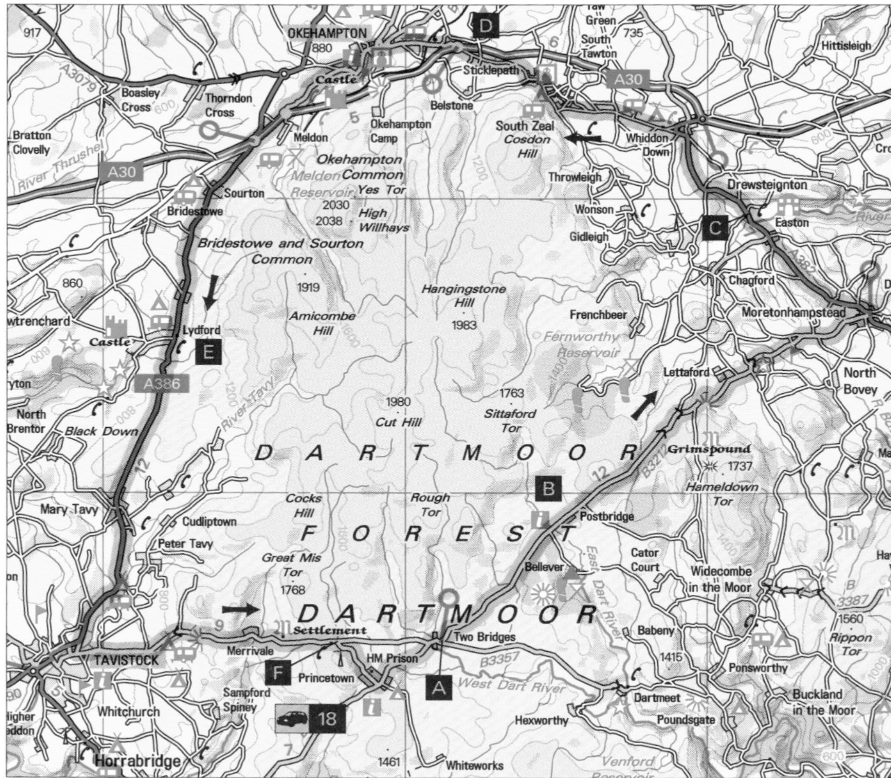

SCALE 1:250 000 OR 1 INCH TO 4 MILES *1 CM TO 2.5 KM*

and Crockern Tor to the left. After the Cherry Brook Hotel you will see the Powder Mills to the left. Gunpowder was made here in the nineteenth century, but the surviving cottages now house a pottery. Bellever Forest is now seen to the right. An old quarry makes a pleasant place to park just beyond the bridge over the Cherry Brook.

If you take the turn to the right, just before Postbridge, and drive for a mile you will come to a car park with forest trails and a riverside picnic place close by.

Carry on into Postbridge B. There is a car park with a National Park Information Centre on the left. **A road to Widecombe goes off to the right, but keep on the main road.** This takes you across a rather featureless stretch of moorland, transformed in August when the heather is out. Several disused quarries provide sheltered parking places.

The famous clapper bridge at Postbridge

The Warren House Inn was built in 1845 to serve the needs of the tin miners and replaced a hostelry, known as New House, which had stood close by for a hundred years or so. The first landlord of the Warren House was Jan Roberts, who was also the warrener, hence the pub's name. His original sign read:

Jan Roberts lives here,
Sells cider and beer,
Your hearts for to cheer:
And if you want meat
To make up a treat
Here be rabbits to eat.

Because the thin soil made burrowing impossible for the rabbits, cigar-shaped mounds of earth were excavated by the warrener and entrances made, making it easy for him to net the animals when required.

After the Warren House there is a succession of wonderful views northwards as the road reaches

• PLACES OF INTEREST •

Princetown
The town would be bleak and unwelcoming even without the prison. It stands at 1,430 feet (436 m) and is utterly without shelter. Princetown was the brainchild of Sir Thomas Tyrwhitt who believed that Dartmoor had agricultural potential. He persuaded the Prince of Wales to allow him to try draining and cultivating the wilderness. When this project failed he suggested that a prison be built on the site to accommodate French prisoners of war, then mainly held in hulks moored in Plymouth Sound. Thus, Dartmoor prison was built in 1806 and soon held 7,000 prisoners, American as well as French, after the War of Independence was declared. The prison was abandoned with the cessation of hostilities, but re-opened as a convict prison in 1850.

High Moorland Visitor Centre. The centre uses interactive computers, as well as life-size figures (including Sherlock Holmes), to shed light on all aspects of life on Dartmoor, past and present. Audio visual theatre and art gallery. Open daily Easter–October 10–5. Winter 10–4. Telephone: (01822) 89041.

Wistman's Wood and Crockern Tor
The path to Wistman's Wood passes Crockern Tor. The Stannary Parliament met at this remote spot on at least ten occasions between 1494 and 1703. Ninety-six representatives (twenty-four from each of the stannary districts) would meet at eight in the morning to decide the laws of tin mining and marketing. Crockern Tor was chosen because it was the point where the boundaries of the four stannary districts met. Offenders against the laws were tried at these meetings. If found guilty they were incarcerated in Lydford Castle where they were held in irons and fed only bread and water. In 1532 Richard Strode, the Member of Parliament for Plympton, was thrown into the dungeons for refusing to pay a stannary court fine. He bribed the gaoler so that he was not put in irons or on the bread and water diet. Wistman's Wood is a very sinister place where the last, stunted, oak trees of the original Dartmoor Forest are to be found. It may well have taken its name from the Whisht Hounds, the terrible beasts supposed to roam the moor to snatch the souls of the wicked as they lie on their deathbeds.

The Powder Mills
For information see page 81.

Castle Drogo
For information see page 21.

Museum of Waterpower (Finch Foundary
For information see page 21.

Okehampton
For information see page 21.

Lydford
For information see pages 31 and 32.

Wheal Betsy's engine-house is a poignant monument to a mining industry which disappeared a century ago

the edge of the high moor. Bennet's Cross, to the right, near a small car park, was one of hundreds of similar granite crosses which once marked the pathways across Dartmoor. It is probably five hundred years old, at least. A road to Jurston leaves to the left and, just after this, there is a car park on the left. It is worth stopping here to enjoy the panorama. Landmarks include Castle Drogo, standing above the Teign Gorge and the dome-shaped Kes Tor.

From this point the road begins to descend and crosses a cattle-grid. It passes the Miniature Pony Centre to the right. Take care after the Manor House Hotel as the road will narrow quite suddenly. **Enter Moretonhampstead and bear left opposite the White Horse Hotel, following the signs to Exeter and Okehampton. Turn left again on to the A382 towards Okehampton and the A30.** You will see Castle Drogo ahead. Soon after, the road to Chagford goes off to the left opposite the Easton Court Hotel.

A little further on, opposite the Sandy Park Inn **C**, you can turn right off the route to visit Castle Drogo and Fingle Bridge, a sixteenth-century pack-horse bridge reached from Drewsteignton.

A mile past Sandy Park there is a parking space to the right. A footpath leads to Spinsters' Rock, a Bronze Age burial chamber, denuded of the soil which usually covers these monuments. It is the only one surviving in Devon. Three spinsters were supposed to have built it one night, hence its name.

At Whiddon Down turn left, away from the main A30, towards Sticklepath and South Zeal. Pass Firestone Cross where a lane to Addiscott leaves to the right. Another turn to the right follows signposed to Dishleigh. Almost immediately after this fork right to South Zeal. The village is picturesque, and its inns look as though the coach-and-four could arrive outside at any minute. The Oxenham Arms began life, probably early in the seventeenth century, as the home of the wealthy Burgoyne family. However, it was an inn when Charles Dickens, on a journey to Plymouth, was snowbound at South Zeal. He spent his time writing part of *The Pickwick Papers* there. South Zeal was built in the thirteenth century by the local landowner, but never flourished in the way he had hoped. However, its medieval layout can be clearly seen. Ancient houses are set back from the main street, which widens to form a market-place around a small chapel.

Pass through the village to reach a crossroads. Turn left here to reach the main road and then right into Sticklepath D. The National Trust's Finch Foundry is to the left. **Go straight over the crossroads, with Belstone to the left and Sampford Courteney to the right. Cross the A30 and follow the B3260 and signs to Okehampton town centre.**

Follow the main road through the town until you eventually meet the A30. Take this road heading for Launceston and Tavistock. Shortly after this take the A386 by forking left at Sourton Cross. You can make an interesting diversion to visit Lydford by turning right just before the Dartmoor Inn **E**.

After this the main road climbs up on to the open moor and you can see Brent Tor romantically

South Zeal was once an important main-road village

topped by its lovely church. Another romantic ruin is the remains of Wheal Betsy's engine house, to the right of the road. This is a reminder that, in the mid-nineteenth century, this area with its rich deposits of copper, tin, lead and silver, was the Klondike of Dartmoor. Wheal Betsy was a silver and lead mine. Its engine house was built in 1867, lasting just ten years before the mine was abandoned. There is a parking area close by giving access to beautiful moorland footpaths. Gibbet Hill, to the west of the road, is a fine viewpoint.

If you do not intend to visit Tavistock turn left on to the new relief road to reach the B3357 to Princetown. This road climbs up steadily. After you cross the cattle-grid, and as the road levels out, there is a car park to the right. Take time to stop here. There are wonderful views towards the sea. Cox Tor is to the north of the road. Though not very high, this tor dramatically shows the effect of frost weathering on the brittle rock, dolerite. This is a greenish volcanic material which gives the tor its very steep rock faces. Fragments of stone broken off by frost action is known as clitter. The pieces of granite from Staple Tor, the neighbour of Cox Tor to the east, were used to make setts with which streets were surfaced in the nineteenth century. Vixen Tor, whose profile has been compared with that of the sphinx, lies to the south of the road. Technically, it is not a tor, but a rock pile, standing 90 feet (28 m) high, the tallest such structure on Dartmoor. It can be reached from this car park. (Dogs are not allowed on this route.) A public footpath leads directly to it from Merrivale, a mile or so further on.

The road dips into Merrivale. There is parking on a slip road here by the River Walkham. One of Dartmoor's landmarks, the television mast on North Hessary Tor, 688 feet high (715 m), is seen ahead. There is a car park to the right, called Fourwinds, which is useful for those wishing to see the Merrivale antiquities. A tiny school once stood in this car park. It was built for the children whose fathers worked in the King Tor quarry a mile to the south. The quarry supplied granite for Dartmoor Prison and Nelson's Column in Trafalgar Square. **Just after the track to the TV mast turn right F following the B3357 to Princetown.** ■

• *PLACES OF INTEREST* •

Postbridge
It was only in 1792, when the toll road across Dartmoor came into being, that a proper bridge was built across the East Dart River. It replaced the crude, albeit picturesque, clapper bridge which dates from the thirteenth century. The one at Postbridge is the largest on Dartmoor and, even though its design is primitive, it must have represented a considerable achievement when first built. A nineteenth-century writer illustrated the former isolation and backwardness of Dartmoor by saying that he met a man in a remote village who remembered seeing the first wagon entering the place. The force of water it has to resist when the East Dart is in spate has led to the National Park fixing some of its boulders in place with epoxy resin.

Miniature Pony Centre
Situated 3 miles west of Moretonhampstead on the Princetown road. One of the largest miniature pony studs in the world. There are 150 ponies and donkeys as well as other animals. Adventure playground. Open daily except Fridays, Easter–October 10.30–5. Telephone: (01647) 432400

Tavistock
For information see page 22.

Merrivale
For information see page 24.

The town hall at Tavistock, built when the prosperity of the town was at its zenith

• TOUR 19 •

EXETER, CREDITON AND MARDON DOWN

53 MILES - 2½ HOURS
START AND FINISH AT EXETER

Mid-Devon is the least visited area of the county even though its diverse scenery provides a succession of delights. The tour samples a little of this in its early stages. However, the most spectacular part of the route comes later as it follows the north-eastern edge of Dartmoor. Try to find time to see two of Devon's finest churches, those at Crediton and Doddiscombsleigh. The latter has some of the best medieval stained glass in the West Country.

Take the A377 (Crediton road) from Exeter city centre. This follows the east bank of the River Exe and passes St David's Station. **At Cowley roundabout (where the A396 leaves to Tavistock) branch left on to the A377 following the sign to Crediton, and cross the river over Cowley Bridge.** The bridge is situated at the confluence of the Yeo and the Exe. The great brick house overlooking the bridge is Pynes, built c. 1700 by Hugh Stafford. It soon became the home of the Northcote family. The house takes its name from the village of Upton Pynes, reached by turning right in Cowley and crossing the river. It is worth taking this short diversion to enjoy the view from the churchyard.

Stay on the A377 to come to Newton St Cyres. Here a green is overlooked by whitewashed, thatched cottages. The beautiful church, also overlooking the green, is dedicated to Saints Julitta and Cyriac. There is a famous monument to John Northcote who died in 1632. He is brilliantly portrayed, surrounded by his two wives, six daughters, and one cherished son.

Crediton is just over 7 miles from Exeter. In spite of this proximity the main street, nearly a mile long, is lined by good shops. **Keep on the A377 through the town, passing the beautiful church on the right, and following the signs to Barnstaple.** After Crediton the countryside is rolling farmland with fields of

• PLACES OF INTEREST •

Exeter
For information relating to Exeter's historic buildings see page 60 and the city's cathedral page 70.

The Underground passages of Exeter, entrance off the High Street, next door to Boots. The passages were built to bring water into the walled city in the thirteenth century. Visitors are able to take guided tours through these and also visit an interpretation centre. With its low vaults, uneven floors, and dim lighting, this is not an attraction which will appeal to the claustrophobic! Open Tuesday–Saturday Easter–October 10–4.45. Tuesday–Friday November–Easter 2–4.45 and Saturday 10–4.45. Telephone: (01392) 265887 or 265858.

Exeter Maritime Museum, The Haven. Boats from all corners of the world are the main feature of the museum including the world's oldest steamboat. There is a reconstruction of Henry VIII's flagship where children can try hammocks and climb rigging. Open daily April–September 10–5, October–March 10–4. Telephone: (01392) 58075.

Royal Albert Museum, Queen Street. Fine Victorian building. Collections illustrate a wide variety of subjects, local and national. Also fine art galleries. Open all year Tuesday–Saturday 10–5.30. Telephone: (01392) 265858.

St Nicholas Priory, The Mint (off Fore Street). Once part of a Benedictine monastery, the building later became the home of a wealthy Elizabethan merchant. Open Easter–October. Telephone: (01392) 265858.

Topsham Museum, The Strand, Topsham. A late seventeenth-century merchant's house with period furniture and a sail loft. Exhibits illustrate Topsham shipbuilding industry and Honiton lace-making. Open Monday, Wednesday, Saturday, March–November (and Sundays in July, August and September) 2–5. Telephone: (01392) 873244.

SCALE 1:250 000 OR 1 INCH TO 4 MILES *1 CM TO 2.5 KM*

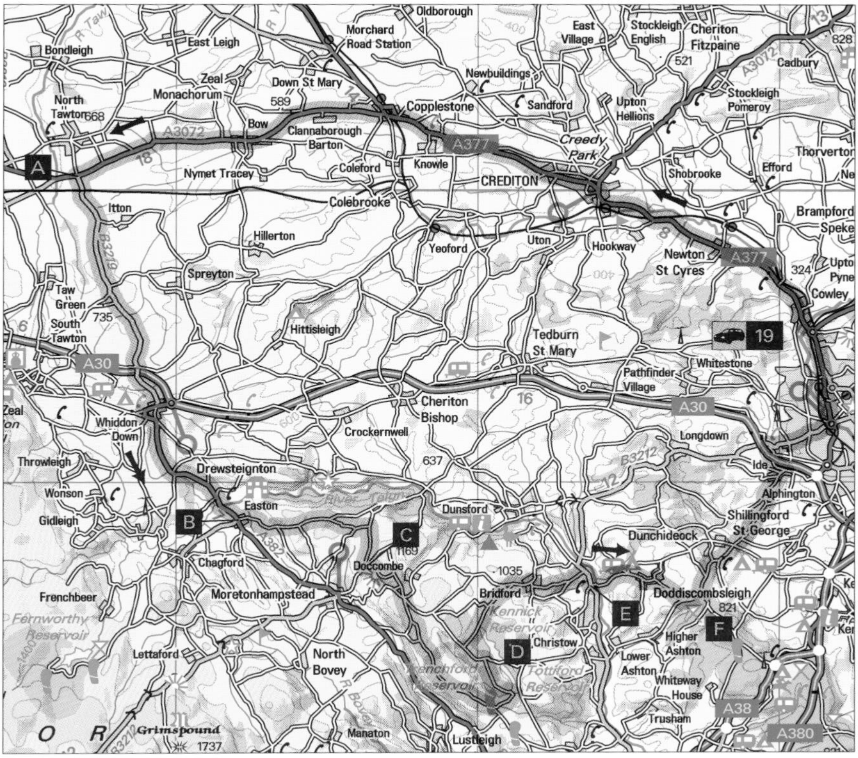

red clay, some of the best farmland in Devon. Dartmoor can be seen on the horizon to the left. **At Copplestone bear left on to the A3072 towards Okehampton.** This village takes its name from the granite pillar which stands at a point where three parishes meet. It is elaborately carved with an interlacing design, and was standing here in 974 when it was mentioned in a charter.

After Copplestone the agriculture is pastoral rather than arable. The village of Bow is another small Devon village which has a French twin – even the humblest villages in Devon seem to enjoy pairing themselves with similar sized villages in France. Originally situated to the south (where Nymet Tracey is today) Bow was established at its present position in 1259 when a market charter was granted. It is a long village lining the main road. There is a bridge over the River Yeo at its western end.

About 3½ miles from Bow leave the A3072 by turning left A at De Bathe Cross on to a road signposted to Whiddon Down and the A30. Go past the Railway Inn and beneath a railway bridge. The

The beautiful Guildhall at Exeter

bridge takes the Halse Moor tramway over the road and was formerly part of the Southern Railway's route from Exeter to Plymouth via Okehampton. The road passes through undulating countryside. A bridge takes the road over the A30 to Whiddon Down. **Turn right at a T-junction opposite the Post Inn on to the A382 towards Moretonhampstead and follow the road round to the left.**

Two miles after Whiddon Down, just as the road comes to a sharp bend there is a turn to the left to Spinsters' Rock, a Bronze Age burial chamber, denuded of the soil which usually covers such a monument. It is the only one surviving in Devon. Three spinsters were supposed to have built it one night, hence its name. After this the road dips through attractive woodland and passes the Great Tree Hotel. The next landmark is the Sandy Park Inn where there is a turn to the left to

Drewsteignton and Castle Drogo. You may care to make a detour if you have not already visited these places.

Otherwise, keep on the main road, cross a bridge, and pass the Mill End Hotel. There is a view of Castle Drogo, dramatically situated on top of the gorge, on the left. **At the next crossroads, where the B3206 leaves to the right to Chagford, turn left B just before the Easton Court Hotel.** This takes you up a very narrow lane which has grass in the middle. You may be nonplussed by the way the lane seems to head for the sheer hillside! However, it swings away and then climbs steeply and steadily. **There is a turn to the right to Howton, but keep on towards Clifford Bridge and Dunsford. The next junction is Uppacott Cross where again you keep straight on.** After about 300 yards (274 m) look for a track to the left, by a trig point, which descends to the sixteenth-century pack-horse bridge, Fingle Bridge. It is possible to park at the beginning of the track from where you can take the Fisherman's Path westwards along the wooded banks of the River Teign to Dogmarsh Bridge below Castle Drogo. An equally enjoyable return to Fingle Bridge can be made on the Hunter's Path on the top of the Teign Gorge. The track also leads to a footpath to Cranbrook Castle, one of three enormous hill-forts built to guard the valley in the first century, BC. It gives panoramic views over much of mid-Devon.

At the next junction fork right towards Willingstone and Clifford Bridge. There is a magnificent view to the right as the lane crests the rise on the flank of Butterdon Hill where there is a stone row over a mile long. **Bear left at the next junction, keeping on the major road. At a T-junction which follows turn right to Moretonhampstead.** This is at Little Wooston Farm. After a cattle-grid the road climbs on to Mardon Down and a road joins from the left from Small Ridge.

Turn right C immediately after this towards Exeter, just before another cattle-grid. There are plenty of places to park here for picnics, wonderful views, and walks on the down. Moretonhampstead, with its church perched on a hill in the middle of the town, provides an attractive foreground for views south-westwards over Dartmoor. **Turn right at the next junction to cross a cattle-grid, now heading for Hennock. Fork left when the road divides, to come to the main Moretonhampstead to Dunsford road. Cross over this towards Hennock and the reservoirs.** Blackingstone Rock is seen to the left. The lane passes Higher Elsford Farm and, after this, there is a forest to the left. Just before the next junction there is a car park and picnic area (with toilets) on the left. There are waymarked walks

• PLACES OF INTEREST •

Crediton

The town takes its name from its river, the Creedy. It stands close to this stream's first bridge, built in Saxon times (the bridge is mentioned in 739). By then Crediton was famous for being the birthplace of St Boniface, fifty years earlier. He introduced Christianity into Central Germany and became the first Archbishop of Mainz. This probably aided the town's development as a centre of religion, and in 909 Crediton was given a bishop, the first of nine to occupy the see before it was moved to Exeter in 1050. However, as recompense for losing its bishop, Crediton was given a large collegiate church.

The plan of the present building reflects this, with the tower crossing separating the large chancel (originally used solely by the resident monks) from the nave. Little remains of this church, however, as most of what we see today dates from the extravagant rebuilding carried out in the early fifteenth century when the wool trade brought Crediton a brief period of prosperity. After the Dissolution the church was sold to parishioners for £200. Its articles stipulate that it should be administered by twelve governors, who still have the power to appoint clergy to the living.

Crediton has suffered many misfortunes through its history. In 1571 and in 1590 bubonic plague struck the town and five hundred inhabitants died on each occasion. Furthermore, like most other market towns in Devon, Crediton was afflicted with frequent disastrous fires. On 14 August 1743, 460 houses were destroyed.

The twentieth century has seen Crediton grow as a dormitory for Exeter but, happily, it has managed to retain the character of a country market town.

Castle Drogo

For information see page 21.

Lawrence Castle

Lawrence Castle is, in fact, a belvedere, or memorial tower. It was built by Sir Robert Palk in 1788 as a monument to his friend, General Stringer Lawrence. The General left Palk his fortune of £50,000 enabling him to buy Haldon House. This vast mansion occupied a site lower down the hill. Most of it was demolished in 1920, apart from one wing, which survives as a hotel.

The tower is triangular and is supposed to be based on Shrub Hill Tower in Windsor Great Park. It is almost hidden by trees which were planted shortly before work on the tower started.

Haldon Forest

For information see page 61.

Moretonhampstead from Mardon Down

around the three reservoirs. These reservoirs, Kennick, Tottiford and Trenchford, were the first to be built to capture the water flowing off Dartmoor for the benefit of the Torbay resorts. They are surrounded by forestry plantations and banks of rhododendrons.

At the junction just after the car park fork left. The road crosses the top of the dam and then a bridge separating Trenchford and Tottiford Reservoirs. **It them climbs a hill through woodland to reach a T-junction. Turn left D towards Moreton-hampstead and then, after ½ mile, right on to an unsignposted lane.** This drops steeply into more woodland. There is a parking place on the right. This is intended for anglers in the Kennick Reservoir which is only a few yards from the road at this point. **At a main road bear right to Bridford. In the village turn to the left, by a bus shelter and just before a small chapel, to follow a sign to Exeter and Chudleigh.** The main part of Bridford is straight on past this chapel, in a cul-de-sac.

From the chapel the road descends into the valley of the Teign. Lawrence Castle can be seen on the skyline ahead. **When you meet the B3193 turn right towards Chudleigh.** Pass a nursery centre which offers refreshment. **Turn left E at the Teign House Inn to Sheldon and Doddiscombsleigh. Cross the river and then an old railway to come to the latter village. Keep on the main road to pass the path to the church on the right, heading again towards Chudleigh and Exeter.** Doddiscombsleigh church has five complete windows of late fifteenth-century stained glass, the best in Devon. The windows are all in the north aisle. The east window showing the Seven Sacraments has delightful little details showing scenes of marriage, baptism, penance etc. The seated figure of Christ dates from 1879 when the glass was restored.

Medieval stained glass at Doddiscombsleigh church

The lane climbs steeply to a T-junction where you turn left. Lawrence Castle is ahead as the road climbs to the ridge. **Turn left F towards Exeter.** However, you could turn right into Haldon Forest should you wish to picnic or visit the Birds of Prey Viewpoint.

The road drops down into Dunchideock. **Continue on the main road into Ide and pass through the village. Turn right on to the B3212 to return to Exeter.** ■

• TOUR 20 •

CULLOMPTON, TIVERTON AND WELLINGTON HILL

53 MILES – 2½ HOURS
START AND FINISH AT CULLOMPTON

This drive takes you through countryside which may be new to many. After visiting Tiverton and nearby Knightshayes Court (a National Trust property famous for its garden) the route meanders along country lanes and climbs to the crest of the Blackdown Hills. After enjoying the wonderful views you wander back to Cullompton through a succession of charming villages.

Take the road signposted to Butterleigh which leaves Cullompton High Street by the Manor Hotel, and head westwards out of the town. The hotel, with its overhanging timber front, dates from 1603. It was built as the home of one of Cullompton's prosperous wool merchants. During the Second World War it served as a rehabilitation centre for injured American soldiers.

After about 2 miles the road comes to a 1-in-5 descent. A little further on it comes to an even steeper descent, 1-in-4, down Newte's Hill. **Follow the road down to Tiverton. At the T-junction turn left and follow the signs to Bickleigh (A396) over two roundabouts. Cross the river and come to a third roundabout. The road to Bickleigh leaves to the left here, but your route turns right to follow the Bampton road (A396) through the town, negotiating several more roundabouts.** This follows the River Exe northwards and crosses the A361. **At Bolham A turn right opposite the Hartnoll Hotel to follow the signs to Knightshayes Court.** The entrance to the famous gardens is to the left. **The lane approaches the dual carriageway again, but turn left at the junction just before the bridge to head towards Chettiscombe and Chevithorne. Take the first turning right after this signposted to Chevithorne and East Mere.**

Chettiscombe is a little village with a stream running through it. Another mile brings you to Chevithorne. The tiny church was built in 1843. The vicarage, behind the church, was designed by William Burges c. 1870 in his characteristic, robust, Gothic style. **Keep on past a turn to the right to Craze Lowman.** The manor house to the left is Chevithorne Barton. It dates from the early seventeenth century when it was the seat of the Francis family.

The lane pursues a very tortuous course for the next 2 miles. **Ignore turnings to the left, pass through a farmyard to come to a major road at Uplowman where you turn right into the village.** Pass the church which dates from the fourteenth century, but was

• PLACES OF INTEREST •

Cullompton Church
The most splendid part of this church celebrates the good fortune of the town's foremost wool merchant in the sixteenth century, John Lane, who died in 1529. The south aisle is dedicated to his memory, and is lavishly decorated with emblems of the industry from which he gained his wealth – cloth shears, ships, and teasel frames which used the barbed head of the weed to raise the nap of the cloth. The fan vaulting of the Lane aisle is exquisite, and was probably copied from the Dorset aisle at Ottery St Mary. The church also has a fine rood-screen which runs right across its breadth. Its tower, 100 feet (31 m) high, was only completed in 1549.

Hemyock Castle
William Asthorpe received a licence to fortify his manor house in 1380, and he added an impressive gatehouse, curtain walls with eight towers, and a moat. Only fragments of the defence-works remain today. The medieval hall has been much altered through nearly eight centuries. However, the site close to the church is interesting and the castle had an exciting history. There are excellent displays explaining the story of the castle and the village.

Open Sundays and Bank Holidays mid-April–September (and Tuesdays and Thursdays in July and August) 2–5. Telephone: (01823) 680745

drastically restored in 1863. **At a crossroads B, turn left towards Westleigh and Holcombe Rogus.** Pass the Redwoods Inn and the post office and go through the hamlet of Whitnage. **Take the first turning right after the chapel down an unsignposted lane.** The lane descends steeply once you have passed a house called Chamberlains. **Turn left towards Westleigh at the next junction and then bear right at Stonesland Cross. At Holbrook Hill turn left and then, almost immediately, right at Highley Farm. After about 1/2 mile bear left to pass Westcott Farm. After negotiating more blind bends you will reach Westleigh.**

Turn left at the T-junction in Westleigh. Follow the road round to pass quarries on the left and come to a major road at Cracker Corner. Keep ahead here following the sign to Holcombe Rogus and Greenham. Soon after this a bridge takes the road over The Grand Western Canal. There is access to the country park from here. **Follow the main road round to the right at the next junction where the other road goes to Holcombe. At the next main road turn right and keep on this for about 1/2 mile to join the A38. Turn left here on to the dual carriageway towards Wellington.**

The Grand Western Canal Country Park, near Tiverton

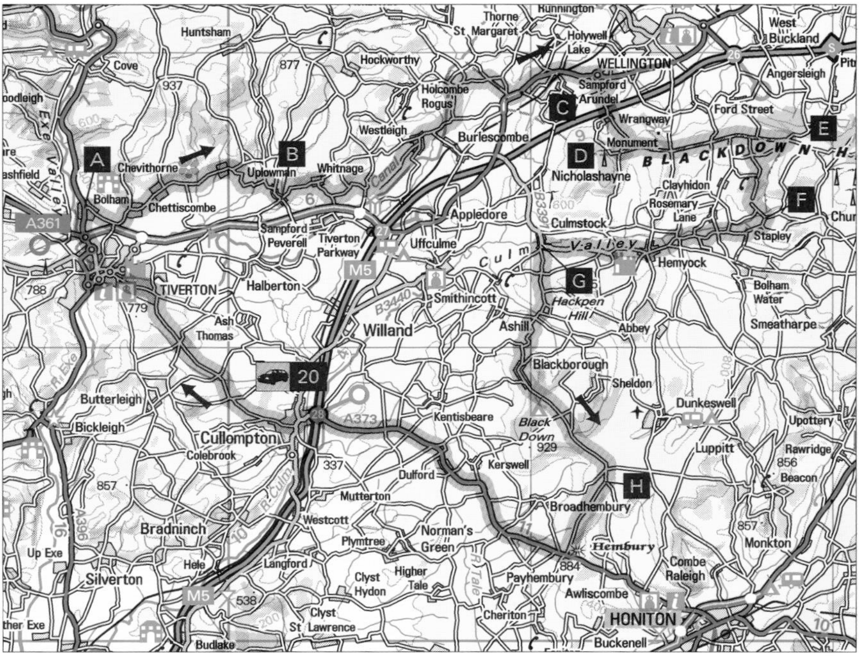

For the next 5 miles the route runs through Somerset. There is a turn to the right to White Ball, a place which gets its name from one of the coloured ball clays to be found in the district. The hamlet of Red Ball is in Devon, about a mile to the south of White Ball. The Blue Ball Inn is also close by in Sampford Arundel, just to the south of the main road. **Keep on the main road to pass the Beam Bridge Hotel and come to a roundabout on the edge of Wellington. Turn right here and then take the first road right following a sign to Wrangway. At the crossroads at Pleamore Cross C turn left towards Uffculme.**

SCALE 1:250 000 OR 1 INCH TO 4 MILES *1 CM TO 2.5 KM*

The road crosses over the M5 and climbs to the top of the ridge. **Follow the main road round a hairpin bend D on to the road running along the top of the Blackdown Hills.** The road to the right goes to Windwhistle Hill, a famous viewpoint which is supposed to allow you to see both coasts of the south-west peninsula. **Keep to the main road which goes through a tunnel of trees.** Just before you get to the next road junction there is a concealed sign on the left of the road which points to a car park and the path to the Wellington monument. The National Trust car park is close to the road here, and people are discouraged from taking their cars closer to the monument. A notice at the monument tells you that a key and a torch are

• PLACES OF INTEREST •

Tiverton

The name of the town derives from 'Twyford', meaning two fords. It was sited at the crossing points of the rivers Exe and Lowman. The earliest, prehistoric citizens occupied a hilltop to the south of the market-place, but in Saxon times a settlement grew up near to the meeting point of the two rivers. However, Tiverton's strategic position was ignored by the Normans (even though its lands were claimed by the king). It was not until the twelfth century that the castle was built by the Courtenays, earls of Devon, who made it their principal seat.

One of the few benefits that these feudal overlords gave to the town was a supply of fresh water channelled beneath the main streets. This was a factor in saving Tiverton from severe outbreaks of pestilence. As in so many other West Country market towns it was the introduction of the wool industry in the late fifteenth century which transformed it from being a drowsy backwater into a busy and prosperous centre of commerce.

Tiverton has an amazing number of ancient charities which were endowed by citizens made wealthy by the wool trade, such as numerous almshouses and the school founded in 1603 by Peter Blundell. It was built to accommodate 150 boys, an exceptional number in those days.

The wealth generated from this trade also gave the town a notable church. It has buttresses bearing carvings of ships which carried Tiverton's goods. John Greenway was one of the most successful wool merchants, and he paid for the south porch of the church and adjacent chapel. These are the most extravagant features of the building.

Tiverton is unique amongst other similar West Country towns in that its wool trade survived the various depressions which killed off its rivals. In 1816 one of the last operating woollen mills was bought by John Heathcoat, a lace manufacturer from the Midlands who had been put out of business by Luddite machine-breakers. He and his successors established a textile industry in the town which continues to this day, though the Heathcoat family is no longer involved.

Tiverton Castle stands opposite St Peter's Church and dates from 1106. One of the circular towers survives from this time with a fine medieval gatehouse. The castle was garrisoned by Royalists during the Civil War, but was eventually taken by the Roundheads. It contains one of the best collections in the country of armour of this period. There is also a fascinating display of clocks. Open April–mid-September Sundays–Thursdays 2.30–5.30. Telephone: (01884) 253200.

Tiverton Museum, Saint Andrew Street. A comprehensive local history collection includes large exhibits such as a Great Western tank engine and farm wagons. Open all year except Christmas week and January Monday–Saturday 10.30–4.30. Telephone: (01884) 256295.

The Grand Western Canal Country Park

This eleven-mile length of canal and towpath must be one of the most remarkable of country parks. The canal was the initial part of an ambitious project meant to link the waters of the Bristol Channel with those of Tor Bay. The project was started in 1810 but was abandoned when the coming of the railways made the scheme commercially unfeasible. However, the section from Cannonsleigh to Tiverton continued to be used until 1925 for the transport of limestone. In 1970 it was decided to preserve the canal as a country park. Its quiet waters provide good fishing and an excellent habitat for birds (kingfishers are often seen), mammals, butterflies, and a wide variety of flora. There is also good coarse fishing.

The towpath gives level walking and access to it from any of the bridges which cross the canal is easy. Access points close to this route are at Great Fossend Bridge at Westleigh and at the end of the canal near Beacon Hill, where the road swings eastwards away from the canal which, at this point, is at the bottom of a deep cutting. Canal Ranger: telephone (01884) 254072.

Knightshayes Court

The house was designed in 1869 by William Burges for John Heathcoat-Amory, grandson of the man who revived Tiverton's textile industry. Unfortunately, the family quailed at Burges' work on the interior and chose a tamer man's designs. The National Trust, in whose care the property has been since 1973, have attempted to restore some of Burges' original work.

The gardens are outstanding, with magnificent trees, rare shrubs, and colourful borders. There are wonderful displays of spring bulbs.

Open April–October daily (but the house closed on Fridays) 11–5.30 (house 1.30–5.30). Telephone: (01884) 254665.

obtainable from the nearby farm should you wish to make the 175-foot (53 m) climb to the top. Following the Duke's victory at Waterloo, the local gentry planned to build this obelisk in his honour. Funds were raised and the foundation stone was laid in 1817, but the elaborate plans soon drained the money, and the monument was left incomplete for many years. The death of the Iron Duke in 1852 brought about the completion of the project.

Go straight over the next crossroads where a road to Hemyock is to the right. There are further parking places as the road heads eastwards along the top of the hills, following the county boundary. **At the Merry Harriers pub turn sharply to the right E towards Clayhidon and then, after about a mile, turn left towards Applehayes and Garlandhayes.** This is a very narrow, twisty lane which slowly descends giving a succession of beautiful views. **Keep on descending to cross a little ford over the River Culm. After this turn right at the top F and keep on to come to a T-junction at Lilleycombe Cross. Turn right to Hemyock.** Pass two turnings to the right going to Rosemary Lane. If you take one of these you will find a roadside memorial to William Blackmore. He was a land surveyor who was murdered at the spot in 1853 for the rents he had collected. The culprit, George Sparks, was soon caught and hanged at Exeter. **At a major road bear right and cross two bridges to enter Hemyock.**

In the main street at Hemyock bear left. Follow the road round so that the church is to the left, following the sign to Culmstock. You will reach this village after a little more than 2 miles. Culmstock's church is unusual in having a tree growing out from the top of its tower. It is said to have taken root here in 1776 when the spire was removed. **Take the turning left to Uffculme in the middle of the village and then, after about 100 yards (91 m), turn left again G on to a minor road following the sign to Dunkeswell. The road to Dunkeswell leaves to the left, but the route continues ahead towards Ashill and Blackborough. Cross a small bridge and turn right and then left to cross a more important lane, still heading for Blackborough.** There are fine views as you come into Blackborough, and even better ones if you walk a few yards along the Bodmiscombe lane, which joins from the left on the edge of the village.

Follow the main road through Blackborough heading for Sheldon and Honiton. The road passes through pleasant woodland where there is a wide choice of walks. Many of the footpaths were made by miners who tunnelled beneath this hill to find Devonshire Batts in its strata. These were whetstones, much in demand when sickles and scythes were used for harvesting. The industry thrived until the invention of carborundum, the last miner giving up in 1929. Badgers and foxes now occupy the labyrinth of old workings.

Ignore a turn to Sheldon on the left and keep on for about 3 miles to go straight over crossroads towards Awliscombe. Just after this fork right H to Hembury Fort. There is more delightful woodland on this stretch of road before you reach the fort, to the left as you come to the main road.

The Wellington Monument on the summit of the Blackdown Hills

This is the most impressive prehistoric stronghold in Devon. It has a succession of ramparts and deep ditches excavated near the end of a steep spur overlooking the Otter valley. The fort dates from about 3300 BC, and its excavation yielded many fascinating finds of weapons, pottery, and other artefacts. Later the Romans utilised the defences of the fort on their first expedition into south-west England.

Turn right on to the A373 and follow this main road to return to Cullompton after about 7 miles. ■

A carpet of Cyclamen at Knightshayes Court

USEFUL ADDRESSES AND INFORMATION

For information on daily events and weather forecasts

Radio Devon 95.8 FM
Devon and Cornwall Weather Forecast Tel: (0891) 500 488 404

Tourist Information Centres

Opening times vary – check by telephone

Axminster
The Old Courthouse,
Church Street, Axminster
EX13 5AQ
Tel: (01297) 34386

Brixham
The Old Market House,
The Quay, Brixham TQ5 8TB
Tel: (01803) 852861

Budleigh Salterton
Fore Street,
Budleigh Salterton EX9 6NG
Tel: (01395) 445275

Crediton
Market Street Car Park,
Market Street, Crediton
EX17 2BN
Tel: (01363) 772006

Dartmouth
11 Duke Street,
Dartmouth TQ6 9PY
Tel: (01803) 834224

Dawlish
The Lawn, Dawlish
EX7 9PW
Tel: (01626) 863589

Exeter
Civic Centre, Paris Street,
Exeter EX1 1JJ
Tel: (01392) 265700

Exeter Services
Sandygate (M5),
nr Exeter EX2 7NJ
Tel: (01392) 437581 or 79088

Exmouth
Alexandra Terrace,
Exmouth EX8 1NZ
Tel: (01395) 263744

Honiton
Dowell Street East Car Park,
Honiton EX14 8LT
Tel: (01404) 43716

Ivybridge
South Dartmoor TIC,
Leonards Road,
Ivybridge PL210SL
Tel: (01752) 897035

Kingsbridge
The Quay,
Kingsbridge TQ7 1HS
Tel: (01548) 853195

Okehampton
3 West Street,
Okehampton EX20 1HQ
Tel: (01837) 53020

Ottery St Mary
The Old Town Hall, The Flexton,
Ottery St Mary EX11 1DJ
Tel: (01404) 813964

Paignton
The Esplanade,
Paignton TQ4 6BN
Tel: (01803) 558383

Plymouth
Civic Centre, Royal Parade,
Plymouth PL1 2EW
Tel: (01752) 264849 or 264851

Salcombe
Council Hall, Market Street,
Salcombe TQ8 8DE
Tel: (01548)843927 or 842736

Seaton
The Esplanade,
Seaton EX12 2QQ
Tel: (01297) 21660 or 21689

Sidmouth
Ham Lane,
Sidmouth EX10 8XR
Tel: (01395) 516441

Tavistock
Town Hall, Bedford Square,
Tavistock PL19 0AE
Tel: (01822) 612938

Teignmouth
Sea Front,
Teignmouth TQ14 8BE
Tel: (01626) 779769

Telegraph Hill
A380 (Top), Kennford,
nr Exeter EX6 7YW
Tel: (01392) 833559

Tiverton
Phoenix Lane,
Tiverton EX16 6LU
Tel: (01884) 255827

Tiverton Services
Junction 27 (M5),
nr Sampford Peverell EX16 7SB
Tel: (01884) 821242

Torquay
Vaughan Parade,
Torquay TQ2 5JG
Tel: (01803) 297428

Totnes
The Plains,
Totnes TQ9 5EJ
Tel: (01803) 863168

Other useful organisations

The Countryside Commission
John Dower House,
Crescent Place, Cheltenham,
Gloucestershire GL50 3RA
Tel: (01242) 521381

West Country Tourist Board
60 St David's Hill,
Exeter, Devon EX4 4SY
Tel: (01392) 76351

Ordnance Survey
Romsey Road, Maybush,
Southampton SO16 4GU
Tel: (01703) 792912

National Trust Regional Office
Killerton House, Broadclyst,
Exeter EX5 3LE
Tel: (01392) 881691

INDEX